ALSO BY RAMESH SHARMA

America Tattwamasi
America Arise and Awake
America Thy Simmering Agony

AMERICA
FACE DOWN
EVIL

RAMESH SHARMA

authorHOUSE®

AuthorHouse™
1663 Liberty Drive
Bloomington, IN 47403
www.authorhouse.com
Phone: 833-262-8899

Published by AuthorHouse 11/27/2020

ISBN: 978-1-6655-0927-5 (sc)
ISBN: 978-1-6655-0926-8 (e)

Library of Congress Control Number: 2020923636

Print information available on the last page.

Thou shalt not be content with the
Kingdom of God on earth
Thou shalt create the Empire of Truth
both on earth and space

Excerpt from
AMERICA THY SIMMERING AGONY

CONTENTS

1. America, Rise, Rise, Rise! 1
2. Purity Of American Soul 2
3. I Am Love 4
4. I Don't Want To Live 5
5. Life, An Addiction 6
6. Man, A Hummingbird 7
7. Mischiefs Of Tiny Brooks 8
8. O Agony! 9
9. O America, Pray Lead Us 10
10. What I Hanker For 11
11. Bravo, America! 12
12. American Lion Mocked 13
13. Darkness Veiled In Darkness 14
14. I Am Storm 15
15. I Want To Flirt With Death 16
16. I Can Even Question 17
17. It Is The Meaning That Counts 18
18. *Prakriti* Running After *Purusha* 19
19. A Scientist Intrigued 20
20. I Will Be Relishing You 22
21. What An Ecstatic Philosophy! 23
22. As None But Yourself 24
23. To All Living On This Planet 25
24. Making A Difference 26
25. This Is What My Conscience Says 27
26. As If It Were A Tiny Earth 28
27. History Is The Mirror Of Time 29
28. Impeach Forty Five 30
29. Postman 37
30. I Don't Want To Waste My Time 38

31. You Must Have Known The Key 40
32. Who Is A Fascist …? 41
33. I Am Rock 44
34. I Dare You To Ask Your Own Being 45
35. Without Any Stigmas 46
36. Just Like Water 47
37. History 48
38. Enjoy It As Much As You Can 49
39. Aren't Success And Failure The Same? 50
40. Go Away 51
41. I Feel Like Writing Something 52
42. O Children Of Universal Consciousness! 53
43. I Am A Rebel 54
44. I Relish The Nudity Of Sun 56
45. Where Do We Come From? 57
46. What Is The Point? 58
47. Death Is Not Invincible 59
48. Let Me Die Pure 60
49. Secretive Dragon's Lethal Gift 61
50. I Am A Bridge 64
51. Is Absolute Neutrality Possible? 65
52. Spread Your Wings 66
53. To Me 67
54. Explode Once Again 68
55. O Evil Incarnate, With Blood Your
    Hands Maligned! 69
56. It Is Time We Prayed 77
57. I Can See Your Reflection 78
58. Great Poetry 79
59. Blood Of My Soul 80
60. Let's Take A Vow 81
61. Our Victory Is Guaranteed 82
62. Could You Please …? 83

63. It Was A Nasty Dream 84
64. Poetry Is A Vibrant River 86
65. How Can You Forget The Glorious Moments?...87
66. How Long Shall I Remain Confined? 89
67. Fellow Religionists 90
68. One Cannot Break 92
69. They All Enjoy 93
70. Silence Of The Meek...94
71. Would You Please Rescue Me?...........................95
72. Whisper Of Silence...96
73. Fire Of *Karma*..97
74. You Are Law Unto Yourself 98
75. O Youths Of China, *Uttishthata, Jaagrata!*...........106
76. Anticipation I Harbor.......................................109
77. Let's Rise To The Occasion! 111
78. Vibration Of My Desire.....................................113
79. Power Of Soul American 114
80. I Salute Your Exceptional Poise 115
81. I Won't Forget You 116
82. A Beautiful Melody 117
83. My Own Stamp..118
84. Even Amidst … 119
85. Why Can't You Escape?.....................................120
86. Never Shall I Vanish..121
87. I Am The Ultimate History 122
88. Nature's Intoxicating Panache 123
89. When Were You Betrothed To Me? 124
90. I Tend To Forget 125
91. May I Know What It Is!......................................126
92. What Good Is Power?...128
93. Let The Paradigm Shift......................................129
94. Silence Rains Disaster..130
95. To Some Life Is Just Like A …...........................131

96. Happy To Trade My Blood 132
97. How Beautiful! 133
98. May You Bless My Fellow Beings 134
99. I Have Sown Its Seed 135
100. Complaint Of A Flower 136
101. Time's Fourth Child 137
102. Again In Their Lives 138
103. How Can I Express? 139
104. I Don't Know Why My Emotions … 140
105. With Dreams Marigold 141
106. Nor Shall Ever Be 142
107. Dewdrop 143
108. Sharing Agony 144
109. Heart Pierced 145
110. Thou Shalt Never Bow 146
111. Spooky Entanglement 147
112. Dystopian Vortex Of Red 148
113. Never Perturbed 149
114. Why Is My Heart So Thirsty? 150
115. Help Me Remove 151
116. Music Of Poise 152
117. I Want To See You 153
118. Destroy Demonic Mania 154
119. Tireless Traveler 156
120. Now Is The Time 157
121. I Have Yet To Summon 158
122. America, A Blessed Land 159
123. Bright Dreams And Terrible Nightmares 160
124. Don't Ever Let My Country Dissolve 162
125. I Am A Child 163
126. We Are All Students 164
127. Absurd Paradoxes 165
128. A Luminous Streak 166

129. Let The Soaring Bird Take Rest 167
130. Vibrate, O My Soul! 168
131. Why Should I Be Gratuitous?................................169
132. What A Bizarre Anomaly! 170
133. Could You Learn Something? 171
134. Let Us Pursue 172
135. Where Is Truth, Beauty And Bliss? 173
136. They Are All Divine Vibration 175
137. I Do Celebrate The Unity 176
138. Light Of Freedom And Divinity............................177
139. Who Is Not touched?...179
140. Radiant Is Your Realm 180
141. Gita's Immortal Message To The
     Youth Of World 181
142. Do I Cherish You..183
143. No Matter How …...184
144. You Have Enveloped 185
145. I Am Infatuated 186
146. You Are The Mightiest Warrior 187
147. An Unassuming Bard 188
148. May I Savor The Exhilaration 189
149. Haven Of Beggars...190
150. O Brave Soldiers …..192
151. Nocturnal Predator 193
152. Let Me Vanish 194
153. Is There Another World Beyond? 195
154. O Immortal Heroes Of America!...........................196
155. Let Not My Thirst Be Quenched! 199
156. I Am Not Interested 200
157. A Prayer 201
158. How Beautiful A Coexistence!..............................202
159. Poor Robots!...203
160. I Might Sound Weird 204

161. 'Yeast Of The Pharisees' 205
162. Reduced To An Inanimate Chariot 206
163. Continued To Flow 207
164. Marbles Of Words...208
165. I May Not Have To … 209
166. Don't Worry..210
167. The Language Of Life 211
168. The Labyrinth Of Illusion.....................................212
169. Full Of Dark Paradoxes.......................................213
170. Eternal Roar Of Human Soul...............................214
171. Frown 215
172. A Life Infuriated...216
173. Bloodthirsty Specter..217
174. Cherishing My Love...219
175. Amorous Touch..220
176. Alter Ego Of Cruel Destiny 221
177. Tears And Loneliness... 223
178. Let Not Your Life Dissolve 224
179. Hold Back Just For A Moment 225
180. Divinely Invincible 226
181. A New Perspective 227
182. Woe To The Regimes! 234
183. Eternal Urge Of Human Existence......................235
184. Relation With Our Shadow 236
185. A Moment With Fear..237
186. A Moment With My Tears 239
187. A Moment With Time 241
188. Thou Art The One 243
189. Aesthetic Echo...244
190. Harbinger Of Armageddon..................................245
191. I Am The Source 246
192. Joy Of A Big Family...247
193. Billowing Black Clouds.......................................248

194. Let Birds Fly 250
195. Born Free...251
196. Pearls In Oyster Shells 252
197. "Thou Shalt Not Fear Death" 253
198. Keep On Pronouncing 254
199. Try Not To Fool Yourself....................................255
200. Not A Whim..256
201. Tyranny Will Kneel 257
202. Just Learn..258
203. Whom Shall I Ask? 259
204. Just Like Fossils..262
205. Let Me Experience Democracy 263
206. I Can't See 264
207. O Priests Of Democracy And Freedom! 265
208. Let's Explore The Bright New World 267
209. Competing To Elope...268
210. Incarcerated For Centuries 269
211. Pray Lead Me 271
212. Plight Of A Widow 272
213. Meditation...273
214. Never Shall I Cease To Enlighten 275
215. One With Her 276
216. Sometimes I Dive Deep … 277
217. Just Like A Bumblebee..278
218. Central Message Of My Cherished Book 279
219. A Tiny Moment
     I Want To Spend With Myself 301
220. Thine Is A Pyrrhic Victory! 307

AMERICA, RISE, RISE, RISE!

America,
Rise, rise and rise
Just keep rising, rising and rising
Infinite is your journey
Unimaginably far your destination
Heed the echo coming from across the cosmos
As if beckoning you to join its universality
Pursue the injunction of the Intelligent Supreme
Who wants to share his transcendence with you
Immanent you are in every dimension of existence
As inexorable urge for freedom and liberation
America,
Rise, rise, rise
Just keep rising, rising and rising
Along with you will exalt the beleaguered mankind
And humanity will find itself graciously consecrated

PURITY OF AMERICAN SOUL

O America,
How can your offspring be Fascist?
Isn't it a sin to hurl such an epithet at them?

Look,
In their veins runs your blood
In their senses abides your sensitivity
In their mind rests your serenity
In their conscience resides your judgment
In their heart lives your wisdom
And in their Self rests your Soul

O America
The greatest philosophy of freedom and liberty,
The phenomenal expression of the Being Supreme
You are the empirical equivalent of the Absolute
How can your offspring be something otherwise?
Aren't they the *children of bliss and immortality*?

How can someone,
Who believes in the *Unity of Soul*,
Hate others?
Isn't it true
That, as the blessed offspring of yours,
'Universality of Spirit' runs in their veins, too,
In the form of love towards entire mankind?
How can they disparage their own neighbors?
How can they disdain their own fellow beings?
How can they despise their own fellow Americans?

No doubt,

Deceptive modes of Nature
Might have forced them
Into lust, greed and wrath
Certainly this is something,
Ephemeral and transient

The Absolute cannot be blemished
By the anomalies of apparent world
These aberrations, too, can hardly dent
The purity of American Soul

True,
Animus and hatred is alien to their nature

November, 2019

I AM LOVE

Those
Who want
To quench their thirst,
Come to me

Those
Who want
To be intoxicated,
Come to me

Those
Who want
To be lost in ecstasy,
Come to me

Those
Who want
To bathe in bliss,
Come to me

Those
Who crave for fulfillment
And purpose in life,
Come to me

I am Love,
Pure, pristine, eternal,
And infinite

The sole source
Of everything,
Enviable, and worth pursuing

I DON'T WANT TO LIVE

I don't want to live
In a world,
Inhabited by the dead,
And corpses
That make no response,
Even if trampled or crushed
By forces,
Inimical to our existence

I don't want to live
In a society
Where
The decimation of Soul,
And crushing of Conscience
Are readily accepted
As inexorable decree of fate

I don't want to live
In a community
Where
People have their veins,
Overflowing with icy water,
Instead of electrifying blood

LIFE, AN ADDICTION

Like water life is fluid,
and like wind impetuous

An enigmatic blend of
smiles and tears,
agony and ecstasy

Life tends to
intoxicate mortals

It is an addiction,
a deceptive hallucination

The more we get attached to it
The more it spurns us

MAN, A HUMMINGBIRD

Hummingbirds travel
Hundreds of miles at a stretch
Diminutive bodies can't
Keep them from making
Amazing adventures

Undaunted, tireless,
Persistent and unyielding,
Man - a hummingbird
Of this inscrutable universe,
Traverses the length
Of his destiny

Always
Serene, solemn and graceful,
His conscience,
Opens up for him
Umpteen vistas,
Pregnant with the possibility of
Eternal exploration

MISCHIEFS OF TINY BROOKS

Have you ever heard
An ocean complain
About the mischiefs
Of tiny brooks?

Rather she takes
Their frolics as her own
Children's desperation
To dissolve into her lap

Calm and solemn,
She is often seen extending
Her motherly arms wide,
In fond anticipation of their arrival

O AGONY!

O agony,
Why don't you
Flow out these eyes,
So I can drink
Your poignancy
And console myself?

O AMERICA, PRAY LEAD US

O America,
I read the *Bhagavadagita*
In wars you wage
To establish truth and righteousness

I read the *Upanishads*
In your astounding foray into
The world of science and engineering

I read the *Brahmasutra*
In your deep contemplation on
The future of mankind

O America,
A vivid embodiment of
The *Prasthanatrayi,*
Pray lead us to
Truth, light and immortality

WHAT I HANKER FOR

O my Soul,
I neither disdain the *paigam* of death
Nor do I hanker for the *tawaza* of life
Your *aashraya* do I fervently seek
Where I can find myself merged
In eternal beauty and sublime bliss

BRAVO, AMERICA!

Bravo, America!
Thy hands those of goddess *Durga*
Killing the despicable monster, *Mahishasura*

Qassem Soleimani is dead
The world has got rid of terror
Unprovoked death of hundreds of thy brave sons has
    been avenged
Allies heave a sigh of relief
Despots, dictators and tyrants suffer dreadful
    nightmares

America,
In thy extraordinary decisiveness
Is hidden the quest for righteousness,
And in thy unparalleled strength
Relentless search for truth and justice

A momentous lesson,
Theocratic Mullahs of Iran
Can ignore at their own peril -
Behave, enjoy the blessings of merciful Lord
Or else, for extinction get yourself prepared!

January, 2020

AMERICAN LION MOCKED

Today,
I was really amused
To see the mighty American Lion
Mocked by rapacious
Transatlantic hyenas, along with
Their Canadian buddy,
Over their dismal failure
To snatch former's
Delectable kill

Not surprisingly,
The muckraking hyenas'
Craven smirk
Delighted servile vultures,
Hellbent on dislodging
The King of the Forest,
With ludicrous, and
Fake screams

December, 2019

DARKNESS VEILED
IN DARKNESS

Darkness
Wrapped up in darkness

Incarcerated behind the Stygian darkness
Were both existence and non-existence,
With their urge for Freedom suppressed

Suddenly the chain was broken,
And from the deep recess of darkness,
Exploded celestial effulgence,
Brightening the entire cosmos -
As if it were Freedom's exhilaration
At its own birth

Theatrics followed by enchanting sound,
Vibrating the cosmos with Elysian melody

Along with the birth of Freedom,
Thus manifested
Both existence and non-existence

Who was behind this heavenly drama?

Perhaps none,
Other than my own Self,
Also celebrated as the Consciousness Supreme

I AM STORM

I am storm
Violent, destructive and apocalyptic,
Meant for annihilating
The illusory spell of *Maya*, and
Attachment to the world of appearance
My mission is to expose mortals
To the true nature of reality,
So they get really passionate
About their freedom and liberty,
Both temporal and spiritual

I WANT TO FLIRT
WITH DEATH

Complete motionless,
I want to travel
across the globe

With my eyes closed
I want to see the light

Without departing from
the embrace of life,
I want to flirt with death

I CAN EVEN QUESTION

O Creator,
I can even question your authority,
And speculate about your existence
I don't need your authorization to do so
My own Soul is powerful enough

IT IS THE MEANING THAT COUNTS

It is the meaning
That counts,
Not words

It is the fragrance
That counts,
Not objects

It is the melody
That counts,
Not notes

It is the Soul
That counts,
Not body

PRAKRITI RUNNING
AFTER *PURUSHA*

Absorbed in deep meditation, *Purusha* seemed lost in
　　himself

Oblivious to the external world, he was perhaps
　　reveling in the realm of nothingness

Suddenly swayed by amatory impulses, *Prakriti* started
　　giving in to coquetry

Perhaps prompted by voyeuristic desires, *Kamadeva*,
　　too, could not resist the temptation of whispering
　　in the ears of *Purusha*

Purusha suddenly found himself awakened to swirling
　　waves of amour inside him

And got engaged in flirtation with *Prakriti* who was
　　sorely cherishing his love

Much to the elation of *Kamadeva*, love between two
　　celestial lovers culminated in the creation of
　　cosmos

The birth of the child was celebrated with
　　unprecedentedly colossal fireworks, followed
　　by the euphonic vibration of Om

As if ashamed at the amour-induced breaking of
　　samadhi, *Purusha* has since been concealing
　　himself behind the world of appearance

Still agitated by insatiable thirst for love, *Prakriti* seems
　　running after the *Purusha Supreme*

We can all feel the ardor of her love in the mesmerizingly
　　dazzling multiplicity of the phenomenal world

A SCIENTIST INTRIGUED

Once somewhere near the event horizon of a massive black hole, a scientist from earth encountered a somewhat strange man with a majestic physique, apparently wearing some divine countenance, exuding the air of sublime serenity.

Since both were curious to know about each other, they started talking after a brief exchange of pleasantries.

The scientist from earth enquired, "You don't look like someone from the earth; may I know actually where you are from?"

The latter replied: "Yes, you are right, I am not from the earth. I am from a different planet, almost half a million light years from your earth."

"Why are you here?" asked the scientist. "What are you looking for?"

"I am doing research on the nature of reality," said the strange man. "Therefore, I am looking for truth."

With his inquisition further inflamed by his response, the scientist went on asking: "May I know what exactly you are expecting to find in this massive black hole to shore up your research on the nature of reality?"

"Yes, certainly I do believe that I might find something here to prove the immortality of human Soul," said the strange man. "The nucleus of this massive black hole could be the key to excavating the truth behind the basic character of human Soul - eternal, infinite and all pervasive."

"I am really confused by your narrative that, to me, sounds rather esoteric and abstruse," said the scientist. "Do you really see any relation between human Soul and the core of this massive black hole?"

"Of course, I do," said the strange man with full confidence. "Even these black holes owe their existence to human Soul. Were it not for human Soul, the cosmos would not be in existence, let alone these black holes."

As the scientist was about to pose further questions, much to his consternation, the strange man suddenly morphed into a flash of deep blue light, and vanished from his sight.

The scientist has ever since remained intrigued by the stranger's theory of relation between the core of black hole and human Soul.

I WILL BE RELISHING YOU

Once I am here,
I will be here forever
Even if I seem to go, I won't
Hiding somewhere
In the loving embrace of Nature,
I will be cherishing and relishing you
Turning myself into a gentle breeze
I will be fondling you
As fragrance of flowers, I will be pleasing you
In the light of moon, you will find me soothing you
In solemnity of ocean, you will find me sobering you
Always shall I be pursuing you as hope, optimism, joy
      and delight
O my fellow beings,
I promise,
I will evermore remain embedded in your urge for
      freedom -
Both temporal and spiritual

WHAT AN ECSTATIC PHILOSOPHY!

A glass of wine,
A mesmerizing philosophy,
With an enigmatic power
To catapult you into wonderful transports, and
To land you in an Elysian realm
Where there will neither be past nor future,
Nor the ugly world to weigh on you
You will be merged in the present and now,
With your Being caressed by their sweet melody
Once you submit to its sovereignty,
You will find yourself turned into *Natra*j,
Dancing to the tune of *Mohini*'s bewitching beauty
A glass of wine,
What an ecstatic philosophy!

AS NONE BUT YOURSELF

If you really want to know me
Look with your own eyes
Not with the borrowed ones
Seemingly a tiny pebble with a turbulent past,
A voice lost in the cacophony of hypocrisy,
A patch of cloud prone to dissipation in no time,
I am an inscrutable enigma,
Surrounding the nature of reality
If you look with your own eyes,
Not with the borrowed ones,
You will know me
As none, but yourself

TO ALL LIVING ON THIS PLANET

To all living on this planet now, and
Those to come in future,
I keep on singing praise
Of your enormous potential,
Inexhaustible energy and admirable insight
These gospels of my Soul,
Sacred tribute to the divinity,
Inherent in your phenomenal existence
Not only now but always,
In future even after my departure,
I will continue to pursue you
In the form of spirit embedded in you all
As hope, optimism, courage and adventure
You will always find me
In solemn silence of your shadows

MAKING A DIFFERENCE

It does not make any difference
Whether or not someone is in your favor
It does certainly make a difference
Whether or not God is in your favor

THIS IS WHAT MY CONSCIENCE SAYS

Don't worry about odds and niceties
No matter how heavy, intricate, complex, byzantine
       and abstruse
As long as you are pure, persevering and intrepid,
Sincerely committed to a noble cause,
You need not demur, hesitate, and be inhibited
Just march ahead, go forward!
Take the lead
God is always there to help you
In every step of your journey
This is what my Conscience says

AS IF IT WERE A
TINY EARTH

Something
Subtle beyond imagination
Imperceptible,   inexplicable,   impalpable,   and
        indecipherable
Perhaps Space and Time only
Can comprehend its enigmatic profundity
My story is an adventurous saga
Of a tiny pebble,
Even after braving
Innumerable tectonic upheavals,
It still remains shiny and amiable
As if it were a tiny earth

HISTORY IS THE MIRROR OF TIME

History is the echo of the past
It is devoid of blemishes,
Anointed with the spirit of Time,
It always speaks the truth
It does not succumb to anybody's whims
Nor does it play valet to rulers,
No matter how great and powerful
Attempts will be made to blandish it
But perpetuity defines its moral strength
That never kowtows to impostors
Seemingly malleable in short term,
History, at the end of the day,
Is always stern, harsh and impartial
History is the mirror of Time
On which reflects the face of Truth

IMPEACH FORTY FIVE

O Lord, You have seen the
wrong done to me;
judge my case.
You have seen all their
vengeance,
all their schemes against me.
Lamentation 3:59-60

Jesus was crucified
Abraham Lincoln, Martin Luther King,
And even Mahatma Gandhi,
The apostle of peace and nonviolence,
Were all assassinated
Were they all wrong?
What crime had they committed?
O humans, why aren't you ashamed of your entrenched
        tradition of ruthless intolerance?
Specially towards those
Who steadfastly stand for truth, justice and
        righteousness,
Who devote their entire life to some noble cause,
And those who dedicate themselves to their people,
        country, and even humans and humanity
Thank God!
Destiny's bestial, tribalist impulse has demurred at
        touching that bar of barbarism
Forty fifth President of the United States has been
        impeached by the House of Representatives
Ironically, for having committed absolutely no crime,
        whatsoever

Replete is human history with innumerable instances
When truth had to suffer brutal persecution at the
    hands of untruth

Donald J. Trump, duly elected by more than six million
    Americans, is punished
Why?
Because he loves America and the Americans
Because he is determined to dismantle the entire
    scaffolding on which stands the abhorrent edifice
    of rampant corruption, and misuse of power
Because he seems committed to exposing the
    malfeasance of politicians and their cohort,
    associated with so-called establishments
Because he is determined to drain the 'swamp' that
    has long been gnawing into the vitals of our
    Constitutional Republic
Because under his sagacious leadership, America has
    achieved momentous economic boom, never
    experienced in past several decades
Because his economic policies have resulted in
    unimaginably record numbers of reduction in
    unemployment, and creation of employment for
    Hispanic, African and Asian Americans, and
    women in workforce
Because he seems exceptionally adept at preserving
    and promoting our economic, financial and
    trade interests, based on fairness and reciprocity,
    vis-a-vis other countries of the world
Because he is vehemently opposed to political
    establishments' longstanding policies of giving
    precedence to our adversaries' interests over our

own political, economic and strategic needs and imperatives

Because, unlike some others, he does not even think of enriching himself and his family by using as a leverage American taxpayers' hard-earned money while bargaining with foreign governments

Because he does not sacrifice America's vital security and strategic interests in return for our arch rival's compromising favors, no matter how enticing

Because he is probably the only President in more than six decades who could really stand up to totalitarian regime of China, an enemy, deceptively engaged since long in undermining our vital economic and strategic interests

Because he is the only President in last seventy years who has been able to make the Stalinist regime of North Korea feel the real pain of our punitive strength

Because it is only under his iconoclastic leadership that it has been possible for America to keep itself from being swindled by transatlantic allies

Because he is not prepared to kowtow to callous dictators and theocratic fanatical mullahs

Because he is committed to the uplift of our veterans, and tens of millions of people, virtually abandoned by previous administrations

Because he wants to stop lethal enemies, including terrorists, and members of drug cartels and violent gangs, from pouring into our country

Because he wants to stop the infusion of narcotic drugs and illicit substances into our communities, which is responsible for killing tens of thousands of Americans every year

Because he is uncompromisingly opposed to the policy of an open border, susceptible to the uninterrupted influx of illegal immigrants and criminals from across the globe

Because he is vehemently opposed to the notion of Sanctuary State that, more than anything else, willfully harbors alien criminals, determined to wreak havoc on American societies

Because he is committed to bolstering our law enforcement agencies to make sure that America and Americans are safe

Because he is diehard against providing entire welfare benefits, including free health, free education and free housing, to illegal aliens at the expense of hardworking American taxpayers

Because he is not prepared to deprive millions of Americans of jobs and opportunities by giving in to sinister partisan agendas of so-called scientists and their political collaborators

Because, unlike his predecessors, he gave a new and positive direction to American justice system, by enacting criminal justice system reform

Because he has intuitive brains and guts to discern the underlying intent of our friends and allies, in their approach to our power and position

Because neither political correctness nor political grandstanding can make him swerve from his avowed commitment to America and the Americans

Because he seems bent on destroying the legacy of
ignominious past that would revel in apathy,
apology and appeasement

Because he is steadfast in upholding our Constitution
and the Declaration of Independence, both in
letter and spirit

Because he is determined to protect and promote our
sovereignty, national integrity and independence

Because he wants the entire country to honor the
American flag as a respectable symbol of our
peace, unity and harmony

Because he wants to make America a great country,
worthy of commanding respect and honor of the
entire world

How unfortunate an incident!

Besmirching the history of this great nation

With abhorrent smear, inveterate vendetta and
pathological hatred

America, a respected beacon of justice and rule of law

Suffering brazen violation of fairness and due process

Amidst majoritarians' *ad hominem* assault on the Chief
Executive

Predictably, just like the Great Savior,

A messiah, crucified in Calvary of the House

Resurrected from the Tomb of Senate

With unimaginably enhanced

Grandeur, glory and grace!

No doubt, stained he was forever,

Like *Neelkantha*,

Who, in a bid to safeguard the world from being
annihilated, gleefully swallowed the most lethal
poison, *halahal*

Given the pernicious atmosphere, vitiating our politics
and the entire thinking process, the application
of the impeachment provision should hardly
stun anyone

What is really shocking is the bizarre desecration of
our beloved Constitution, and the lofty ideals,
underlying this sacred document

That the piety of our Statute should be trampled
unceremoniously under the visceral boots of
vileness, vengeance and vendetta, is in itself an
egregious shame

Now even the Souls of our great Founders have no
choice, but to accept it as an ominous *fait accompli* -
an arrow piercing the heart of their momentous
sacrifice and dedication to the cause of truth,
justice and righteousness

O detractors of truth, justice and righteousness,

Just like manic *Duryodhana*, who was perturbed at
the failure of a series of conspiracies, aimed
at destroying *Pandavas*, you seem obsessively
agitated

Regardless of our positions, we are all puppets at the
hands of Time, whose *diktat* no one can defy

Try to comply with his injunctions,

And maintain the decorum of your position

Victory or defeat

History will judge you, based on

How you react to specific defining moments

Because you are a Lilliputian entity

In the greater scheme of things

Your tantrum, however vicious,

Cannot dent the spirit of Time

Shred malice and animosity,
Constantly putrefying your judgment
Shred vendetta and vengeance,
Ceaselessly clouding your vision
Shred rancor and bitterness,
Persistently fouling your approach
Shred animus and hatred,
Ominously spoiling your conduct
O *soi disant* custodians of our future,
Don't ever dare shred the destiny of great country
      America, and brave Americans

February, 2020

POSTMAN

O Postman,
You don't know for yourself
Whether you are carrying the message of happiness
Or the tidings of misery
You are just a carrier
As impartial, detached and indifferent as my own Soul
Which although lifting the burden of my body
Always manages to steer clear of my prejudiced
      existence
Just like my Soul
You connect me with my fellow beings,
And lead towards an enlightened universe

I DON'T WANT TO WASTE MY TIME

Stars, planets, sun and moon
Always keep whispering
Life on earth is too short
To be wasted for nothing

I don't want to waste my time
Writing poems on kisses and lips
I don't want to waste my time
Cherishing buttocks and thighs,
Breasts and hips

I don't want to waste my time
Wading in obscenity and smuts,
I don't want to waste my time
Always pretending to promote
Aesthetics and arts

I don't want to waste my time
Wallowing in trifles of politics
What use is one's ingenuity
Delving into vile derelicts?

What I really want
Is to fortify my core,
So I can gleefully say 'come in'
When Grim Reaper comes
And knocks on my door

I don't want to waste my time

Doting on knickknacks' atoll
One thing I mustn't forget
Infinity is my destination
And eternity my goal

YOU MUST HAVE
KNOWN THE KEY

O America,
The enlightened source of life and immortality,
You must have known the key
To defeating death and its terror
By embracing freedom and liberty
As the heart and soul of your empirical existence,
You have illumined the path
Leading mankind to their true destination
You have raised the onus of escorting human beings
To the Elysian land of peace, prosperity and happiness
You have offered to sail tortured humanity
Across the turbulence of unceasing miseries
O America,
The sole savior of the mortal world,
Certainly, you must have known the key
To defeating death and its terror

WHO IS A FASCIST ...?

O my Soul,
I am confused
Who is a Fascist?
Who is a White Nationalist?
Who is a White Supremacist, and
Who is a Nazi?

I am completely bewildered
By the cacophony,
Arising from recriminations,
Reverberating the ambience
Of this home of the brave

I am egregiously shocked
By the accursed and profane epithets
Being hurled at each other,
Specially among the elites
In this land of freedom and liberty

I don't know
Who that unseen power is
That pulls the string, and
These living puppets start dancing
To the tune of devilry and vileness

I don't know
Who is instigating them
To ditch their own conscience, and
Blare out ominous trumpets
Of race and color

O my Soul,
I know this is the land
Where the sacred mantra
Of *'We the People'*
Was first pronounced

This is the land
Where it was first recognized
That *'All men are created equal'*

And this is the land
That had willingly taken the vow of
'Universality of Spirit'

I do confess
We had committed
Serious aberrations
In the past, and
We should not forget
We have already paid dearly
For what we did

I am really confused
Why we are now so obsessed with
The penchant for
Exhuming the stinking corpse
Of race and color

What is it
If not the perversion
To savor putrid miasma,
Stemming from smear, vengeance and hatred,
Vitiating our body politic?

Why can't we
Think in terms of
Love, compassion, fellowship,
Brotherhood and cohesiveness, instead?

O my Soul,
I am really scared
The demons of race and color
Seem inclined to create
A *'Devil's Island'*
Where our freedom and liberty
Might forever be incarcerated

November, 2019

I AM ROCK

I am rock of the mountain
Snow of the glacier I am
Yet, as generous as the fountain
Is my heart sublime

I DARE YOU TO ASK YOUR OWN BEING

Why has politics become so mean?
Except hatred, vengeance and smear
What can a citizen from it glean?

Why has politics become so mean?
Misuse of power, corruption and loots
Alas, *vox populi* crushed under boots!

Why has politics become so mean?
Appeasement, sellout and kowtowing
O so-called representatives of the people,
I dare you to ask your own Being

WITHOUT ANY STIGMAS

O my Soul,
Where is thy destination,
And how far is thy journey?
Even Time and Space can't
Fathom the intent of thee
Thou art really full of enigmas,
How perfect thou art, absolutely
Without any stigmas!

JUST LIKE WATER

Just like water
I go on changing
My name and form
But never do I vanish
Infinite is my journey
And eternal my wish

HISTORY

History has never been
Anybody's valet
Neither has it succumbed
To anybody's whim

ENJOY IT AS MUCH
AS YOU CAN

Sweet as empyrean nectar,
Seductive as the beauty of celestial nymphs,
Ambrosial as the fragrance of flowers,
Life is really a precious blessing
Enjoy it as much as you can
Remember, it is as much appealing
As it is addictive
Just like opioids,
It might presage your destruction, too
Never submit to its intoxication
Tena tyaktena bhunjitha

AREN'T SUCCESS AND FAILURE THE SAME?

What is success?
And what is failure?
Aren't both of them the same?
What is the color of success?
And what is the color of failure?
If they both are colorless,
Aren't both of them the same?
How much does success weigh?
And how much does failure weigh?
If they both are weightless,
Aren't both of them the same?
What is the height of success?
And what is the height of failure?
If they both are devoid of any height,
Aren't both of them the same?
Where does success live?
And where does failure live?
If they both have nowhere to live,
Aren't both of them the same?
How does the grave define success?
And how does the grave define failure?
If the grave does not make any distinction between
success and failure,
Aren't both of them the same?

GO AWAY

Go away, go away
Hate, malice and jealousy
Don't ever touch my nerve
O ignoble fallacy!

I FEEL LIKE WRITING SOMETHING

I feel like writing something,
Transcendental to time, space and causality,
Unsurpassable by stars, planets and galaxies,
More intense than the tiny dot from which exploded
         the universe,
Eternal, infinite and all pervasive
I feel like writing cosmos
I feel like writing my Soul

O CHILDREN OF UNIVERSAL CONSCIOUSNESS!

O Children of universal consciousness,
Why can't you hear the echo of immortality,
Resonating across the firmament of your existence?
Why can't you see the effulgence of infinity,
Illuminating the halo of your existence?
Why can't you feel the blessings of eternity,
Consecrating the grandeur of your existence?

I AM A REBEL

How come a politician becomes a multimillionaire
Once he holds the public office?
Where does his money come from?
I don't think politics is a lucrative business,
Generating millions of dollars
Why is the justice system quiet in this regard?
Isn't such silence a blatant mockery of rule of law,
While the entire public knows
Someone's deep engagement in shady deals?
What is lobbying for other countries, if not a conspicuous charade?
Isn't it a crime to bolster alien powers at the cost of one's own country and countrymen, in the name of lobbying?
I raise not only one, but thousands of questions, relating to misuse of authority and public fund
I also won't cease to raise questions about the money earned by politicians, peddling power, position and influence
I shall inspire entire fellow beings to discharge their duty towards the motherland by doing the same

As a citizen, isn't it my right to know what is going on in my country?
Isn't it my right to know how the hard-earned money of innocent tax payers is being embezzled by some unscrupulous elements?
Isn't it a crime to twist and misinterpret rules, regulations and laws to suit the corrupt disposition of scoundrels?

O America, as an innocent child of yours, I can't help
        expressing that the emperor is naked
I have absolutely no idea about political grandstanding
        and political correctness
If it is a crime to raise such questions, and it is
        punishable by law, so be it
I am ready to be imprisoned for thousands of years for
        questioning the intents and practices that malign
        your respect, honor and dignity, as the living
        paragon of freedom, liberty and rule of law
But it is not possible for me to tolerate
Rule of law trampled,
Freedom incarcerated, and
Liberty persecuted
Yes, I am a rebel, and
Rebellion my *dharma*

March, 2020

I RELISH THE
NUDITY OF SUN

I relish the nudity of sun
Unashamed of anybody,
It does expose itself without hesitation,
And illumines our universe
It never covers its body with the dark
It recoils when the moon
Sometimes tries to eclipse its obscenity
Sun owes its majesty and strength to nudity
Just like sun, death, too, is not ashamed
Of being exposed before anyone
Perhaps that is what accounts for its invincibility

WHERE DO WE COME FROM?

Where do we come from;
And where do we go?
Are we nothing but tantrum,
Gods tend to throw?

Why do we come here;
And why do we go?
Is it really a mystery,
They won't let us know?

Who is God, and
What's our relation to him?
Commanded by whom
Do we submit to his whim?

What is pleasure;
And what is pain?
What is loss;
And what is gain?

Doesn't oscillation
Between the two
Sound like illusion
Or some voodoo?

Who is that power?
And who is that force?
Reducing mankind
To a tame horse

WHAT IS THE POINT?

Sometimes I wonder why I get inclined to peer into
the past

Certain moments fraught with torturous repentance

Some memories drenched with sordid water of
contrition

Unwarranted advances wrapped in emotion and lust

A piece of life overwhelmed by perilous ignorance

A fraction of Time haunted by quest for carnal pleasure

Flirtatious incitement, lustful provocation, induced
engagement

Deadly poison hidden in the attraction of newly
bloomed flowers, and their coquet fragrance

Constant prodding, incessant insistence and amorous
foray into the vulnerable turf of senses

A deadly contraption, coated with celestial ecstasy

Potential agony, cloaked with momentary exhilaration

A reminiscence, full of remorseful convulsions

A tiny chunk of past, potential enough to evaporate the
pleasure of future

What is the point in a mountain lamenting its own
immobility?

Desert complaining about its searing heat?

And the ocean detesting its welling tears?

DEATH IS NOT INVINCIBLE

Power, prestige and position
Jewelry, prosperity and wealth
Crown, palace and kingdom
Beauty, youthfulness and health
Nothing can sway his will
It can neither be intimidated
Nor can death be bribed
Who can escape its wrath?
Even the cosmos has to yield
Yet, death is not invincible
One thing it cannot face
It fears our fearlessness
And kneels for our grace

LET ME DIE PURE

O My Soul,
Let me see pure
Let me smell pure
Let me breathe pure
Let me live pure
Let me die pure

SECRETIVE DRAGON'S LETHAL GIFT

Profoundly exasperated at growing asphyxiation,

Hong Kong rises in prolonged revolt, demanding for democracy and freedom

Monolithic Dragon faces global opprobrium for having dumped more than a million ethnic Uighurs of Xinjiang into virtual concentration camps

Unprecedented punitive pressure by the US administration to abide by the principles of fairness and reciprocity in trade, commerce and investment

Real measures to punish all kinds of malfeasance, including espionage and the theft of US industrial and military secrets

Smoldering popular disenchantment against rampant corruption, and authoritarian regime's steady slide towards pernicious Maoist orthodoxy

Perhaps for the first time in seventy-year history of Chinese communist dictatorship, China was facing seemingly insurmountable overarching challenges

Against such ominous backdrop, suddenly explodes Wuhan, supposedly the Chicago of China, unleashing hitherto unknown Coronavirus

They don't even take any proactive preventative measures so as to stop the deadly virus from spreading to other parts of the world

Enigmatically enough, Chinese authorities spurn timely US good offices, aimed at helping Beijing contain its potential lethal impact

Hundreds of thousands of people get infected by this deadly virus, and tens of thousands die worldwide

Even 'China centric' World Health Organization that initially tries to cover it up, is bound to call it a pandemic

Globalization suffers an unexpected jolt

The world of trade, finance and investment crumbles, raising the fear of another recession

People worldwide are suggested to practice social distancing and confine themselves to their homes

No meetings, no conferences, no interactions, nothing

It seems as if Time itself has come to a standstill

Really a diabolic irony, the totalitarian Dragon seems to be heaving a sigh of relief

Its ordeals are obscured at least for the time being

Indeed, the global conscience has begun to question whether the lethal gift of the secretive Dragon was really adventitious or premeditated

Chinese cannot forget Wuhan for having hosted the Wuchang Uprising that paved the way for the downfall of Qing dynasty

Is it being used today as part of its effort, aimed at undermining US dominance in contemporary world of politics and economy?

Now the ball is in the court of Chinese Communist regime

Truth must come out

Lest the oppressive communist regime should be accused of nothing short of crime against humanity

'Enough is enough' - will be the *cause celebre* uniting
China against the criminal communist tyranny,
long superimposed on the destiny of one and a
half billion innocent people
In this pandemic is reflected the hideous face of cruel
demon, bent on devouring the empyrean world
of freedom, liberty and self-determination
It could be nothing compared to what might unfold in
future, as the world community's intensifying
penchant for freedom and liberty gets more
and more juxtaposed with the ever increasing
megalomania of an atheist Dragon

March, 2020

I AM A BRIDGE

I am a bridge
Connecting past to the present
I want to see future dancing
To the tune of transcendental
Hope, optimism and excitement
Disdain I do some debris
That smack of arrogance and hubris
Despise I do nescience
That conjures up stories of heaven and hell
I do admire the intuition of our ancestors
Who would see us in heavenly bodies
I do commend their divine approach
That would identify us as something,
Ubiquitous, eternal, infinite and indestructible
To them, we were the same as the imperishable
Energy pervading the universe
Verily, Science was born
When proudly they declared 'tattwamasi'
And the same Science, just like a toddler,
Is trying to walk today, holding the finger
Of their exceptional prescience and vision

IS ABSOLUTE NEUTRALITY POSSIBLE?

Is absolute neutrality possible?
If so, why didn't Vyasa applaud the virtues of Kauravas?
Certainly they might have some qualities worth
    admiring
Why did Valmiki desist from hailing best attributes of
    Ravana?
After all, he was no less a formidable king than Rama
Both Mahabharata and Ramayana
Are essentially the depiction of struggle
Between truth and untruth
While upholding truth, untruth inevitably gets
    obscured
Hence the highlighting of Pandavas and Rama
It cannot be misconstrued as being unfair towards
    their nemeses
What is important is truth
And only truth
Nothing else

SPREAD YOUR WINGS

O freedom,
O liberty,
Dismantle the walls that incarcerate you
Destroy the regimes that imprison you
Decimate the systems that enchain you
Demolish the structures that jeopardize you
Devastate the paraphernalia that undermine you
Incinerate the constitutions that circumscribe you
Annihilate the forces that threaten you
Extirpate the elements that conspire against you
O freedom,
O liberty,
Spread your wings
Embrace the entire world
Let mankind realize their inherent plenitude,
And savor the divine fragrance
Of unity among themselves

TO ME

To me,
Each moment is full of wonderment
Each space is full of reverence
Each Soul is brimming with plenitude
Entire creation is ecstatic at the melody of unity
Just like the dark giving way to glowing dawn,
The world of appearance is melting into true realization

EXPLODE ONCE AGAIN

O self-existent void,
Why don't you explode,
And shower the world
With your fullness?

O self-existent void,
Why don't you explode,
And destroy the forces
Inimical to mankind?

O self-existent void,
Why don't you explode,
And decimate the elements
That crush human Soul?

O self-existent void,
Why don't you explode,
And annihilate the powers
That trample on our conscience

O self-existent void,
Explode once again
With the power of Big Bang,
And usher in a new order where
Human Soul and conscience
Will reign supreme

O EVIL INCARNATE, WITH BLOOD YOUR HANDS MALIGNED!

O evil incarnate,
With blood your hands maligned,
Oozing from the Soul of mankind,
In constant torture and agony,
Crying for truth, justice and harmony!

O dreadful monster,
Your realm based on cruelty and coercion,
Ruthlessness and repression
Deception is your philosophy,
And betrayal your principle
Ingratitude is your creed
And imperiousness your ideal

O atheist juggernaut,
Why are you hell bent
On decimating human Soul?

O hideous monster,
I know how horrible
Your regime is!

You claim to
Be the custodian
Of proletariats

You proclaim

Yourself to be the
Champion of peasants

You boast of
Being the savior
Of the oppressed

But I know
How skewed you are
Against them

You don't allow
Them even to speak
Their mind

You blithely
Wallow in their
Blood and sweat

You pretend to
Safeguard the interests of
Workers worldwide

But your conduct
And action speak
Something otherwise

You bolster
The interests of
Prince and princelings

You do nourish
Corrupt millionaires and

Ruthless billionaires

You seem to be
Drowned in corruption
Neck deep

Your realm
Smacks of abominable
Putrescence

Your regime is
Based on devious jehad
Of misinformation

You believe in
Vicious disinformation
Crusade

Yearning for self
Determination is dubbed
Les majesty

Demand for
Democracy considered
Sedition

Cry for human
Rights is nothing
But treason

You pulverize
Their apologists with
Mighty tanks

You treat
Religions as a crime
Against the state

You dump their
Followers in concentration
Camps in the millions

You forbid people
From interacting with
Global community

Afraid that your
Abhorrent excesses might
Get exposed

You incarcerate
Poets and writers,
The conscience of society

You control
The mind of the
People

You
Crush their
Soul

You present yourself
As an ardent advocate of
Peaceful coexistence

But it has proved
Nothing, but a facade to
Mask your hideousness

You conspire
Against nations' urge for
Freedom and liberty

You prop up
Murderous regime of
Stalin's vestiges

You pretend to be
Peaceful, but always keep
Neighbors under threat

You often bully
Them into kowtowing
To your diktat

You intervene
In their legitimate
Rights and interests

You make
Unauthorized inroads into
Their lands and waters

You seem conspiring
Even to turn space and heaven
Into a battleground

You subjugate

An independent state by
Massacring its people

Ruthlessly you
Trample on their culture,
Religion and tradition

You are bent on
Spreading your brutal
Sphere of influence

You stoop so low
As to steal secrets
Of other countries

You defy
The order based
On rules

You suppress
And muzzle media that
Reveal the truth

You don't hesitate
Even to commit crime
Against humanity

You can go even to
The extent of poisoning
World community

You are so unabashed
As to blame others for the

Heinous crime you commit

You are the most
Irresponsible force,
Accountable to none

You are the
Damocles' sword hanging
Over human race

O Monster,
Your regime is a festering
Sore of humanity

Human civilization
Can no longer bear your
Gruesome realm

O world of freedom,
Stand up in unison to
This anathema

O world of liberty,
Wipe it off the map
Of human imagination

It deserves the same
Fate as nazism, fascism
And the evil empire

Eviscerate
This cancer before
It is too late

O monster,
Stop reveling in fiendish fantasy
Free world is not going to be blind and deaf
It will not allow its eyes and ears to be sealed,
Nor is it going to suffer confusion and distraction
Rather it is about to awake
With indomitable will and unyielding determination,
To consign your evil spirit to eternal damnation

Responsible for the horrific murder
Of tens of millions of people,
O disgraced monster of the past,
The Soul of the great civilization,
Along with its innocent people,
Seems desperate to get rid of
Your ominous pall

March, 2020

IT IS TIME WE PRAYED

What has assaulted our mind?
We all seem abjectly sedated
We have lost sensitivity
We have lost our conscience
We fail to distinguish between love and hate
We see friends in enemies, and enemies in friends
We seem disoriented by some black magic
It is time we prayed to the Almighty, and
Invoked the Soul of this great nation

January, 2020

I CAN SEE YOUR REFLECTION

O my Soul,

I can see your reflection in entire object of creation

I can feel you in human emotions, impulses and sensibilities

I can fathom you in their mind and intellect

Even in the silence of objects inanimate, I can feel your solemn presence

I can feel you in the extraordinary order, sustaining the unimaginably vast universe

I know, you are the unity, underlying this phenomenal world of appearance

You are the Supreme magician, playing the magic of names and forms

You are the eternal science on which is based the structure of this universe

You are the superb philosophy that defines the nature of reality

You are the immortal poetry on which are inscribed the emotions of existence

GREAT POETRY

Set yourself free
Unbind yourself
No meters, no rhymes
No phony decoration
Far from the shadow
Of hoary tradition
Give words to your
Emotion and impulses
Give meaning and purpose
To the beauty of silence
Bejeweling your conscience
Write what you want to
Anything that comes
Through your heart
Will make a great poetry

BLOOD OF MY SOUL

I am in the habit
of writing poems
with the blood of
my Soul

My poems can be
violent tornadoes,
devastating the tyranny
of tyrants

They can be
catastrophic
nuclear explosion,
vitrifying
the criminal regimes
of despots, and dictators

Capable of
upending tectonic plates,
they can cause
the death of monolithic
evil empires

Revolutions
of all time owe their
cataclysmic power to the
blood of my Soul

LET'S TAKE A VOW

Fellow Americans,
Arise and awake!
Our existence has been threatened,
Communities shattered,
Economies crippled,
Psyche assaulted,
Conviction challenged,
Principle jeopardized,
Philosophy hammered,
Ideal bludgeoned,
Nations paralyzed
It is really an extraordinary moment
The evil has cast its lethal spell
Environment is poisoned
With deadly virus, hunting us all
Entire world is gasping for life
Isn't it a moment to invoke the State of Unity,
Defined by our inherent trust in human Soul,
And unite the world that believes in
Democracy, freedom and liberty?
It is also a moment of reckoning
Therefore, let's take a vow
Not to rest until the reign of evil
Is razed to the ground,
And entire earth is illumined
With the benign light of freedom and liberty

March, 2020

OUR VICTORY IS GUARANTEED

Entire world seems cringing
Nobody knows,
Where Grim Reaper is peeking from,
And whom he is going to strike
Abetted and intoxicated
By the evil spirit's brimming cup of poison,
He seems excitedly encouraged
To foray into our lives
O my fellow humans,
Let's take it as a test
Of our power, will and strength
Let's face it down
With exceptional strength and fortitude
Come on, let's reflect
We are not born to be defeated
Eternal victory of human beings
Is indelibly inscribed on the pages of Evolution
Even if we are forced to lose our body,
We will evermore live as invincible Soul
Come on, let's challenge it with love,
Compassion and togetherness among ourselves
Our victory is guaranteed
Let's rest assured!

March, 2020

COULD YOU PLEASE ....?

O intelligentsia,

Could you please stop spewing venom against the fundamentals of this great country?

Could you please refrain from engaging in blame game, just to cover up your sick mindset?

Could you please restrain yourself from bolstering arch enemies by undermining our vital interests?

Could you please control yourself from discrediting our reverential institutions?

Could you please hold off peddling poisonous gibberish in the name of ideas and opinions?

O pundits,

I am not asking you to not exercise your rights to free speech and expression

What I am asking you is to abstain from making a mockery of freedom and democracy, by regurgitating rot and putrescence

Please don't ever try to befool Americans whose conscience is far above your malicious buffoonery

March, 2020

IT WAS A NASTY DREAM

As I was heading towards a nearby library,
All of a sudden, I fell into a ditch,
With lots of books and research articles,
Written by great scholars;
Respected periodicals,
With noted university professors as contributors;
Magazines on foreign affairs,
Carrying articles of internationally renowned writers,
And luminaries of intellectual world;
Globally celebrated dailies and weeklies,
Run by professional journalists and famous pundits
I thought I was the luckiest man
To be blessed with precious
Ideas, views and comments of such a highly celebrated
          community
The moment I started reading them,
My heart began to ache,
And my vision got clouded
Bright images moving on the wall
With unbearable cacophony
Would further agonize me
Thinking that I might have some problems
With my own system, I persisted somehow
Much to my anguish and torment,
My whole body,
Along with my conscience started stinking,
And I suffered traumatic suffocation
I did cry and recoil violently to get rid of this hell
Meantime, a German Shepherd appeared,
And rescued me out of the ditch

He didn't stop there,
He began to lick my entire body
Until I was completely stink-free
Once he was done, he gave a short bark
That awoke me to the world of reality
It was all nothing but a nasty dream
The instant I found myself lying on bed,
The clock on the cupboard struck 1 am
I looked out the window
Full moon with her nymphal smile,
Was showering dispassionate love
And soothing calm upon the mortals
But the calendar that carried the portrait of
Saraswati, the Hindu goddess of learning,
Was swaying on one of the walls
Due to unsavory breeze encroaching my room

March, 2020

POETRY IS A VIBRANT RIVER

Poetry is a vibrant river
Let it flow in its own course
Don't ever try to confine it
To a swimming pool,
No matter how luxurious and deluxe
In its serpentine movement is hidden
Exquisite panache of *Prakriti,*
And in its solemn persistence,
Divine virility of the *Purusha Supreme*

HOW CAN YOU FORGET
THE GLORIOUS MOMENTS?

O Free World,

Your confidence in freedom and liberty has been
        challenged

Your commitment to rule of law has been questioned

Your conviction has been dealt a body blow

How did you get yourself caught off guard about the
        biological warfare?

Look, how economies have been completely atrophied

How people in tens of thousands have succumbed to
        deadly virus

How international community has been traumatized

How entire world has been pushed off edge

Ominous enough,

The perpetrator seems defiantly remorseless, and

Unabashedly prone to shift blame

Further threatens to plunge the leader of the Free World
        into the mighty sea of Coronavirus

O Free World,

Destiny seems to have presented you with two
        alternatives -

Either surrender yourself and help the fiendish force
        establish its evil empire on earth

Or get united around the lofty cause of freedom and
        liberty, and exorcize the evil spirit into oblivion

O Free World,

How can you forget the glorious moments when nazism, fascism, and even the seemingly invincible evil empire were all consigned to the trash can of history?

March, 2020

HOW LONG SHALL I REMAIN CONFINED?

O my Soul,
How long shall I remain confined
To the cage of flesh and bones?

How long shall I remain obscured
By false ego and elusive emotions?

Why not enter the sacred temple of
Humanity and chant prayers of humans?

Why not let my effulgence
Illumine the destiny of mankind?

FELLOW RELIGIONISTS

Dear fellow Muslims,
My heart goes to you,
When I see fringe elements
Staining the divine beauty
Of your faith and religion

I find you incarcerated
In damp and gloomy cells
That can hardly see the
Rays of hope and optimism

My dear fellow Christians,
My heart goes to you,
When I find you beguiled
Into equating the Lord's message
With hypocrisy and superstition

I find you groping in the miasma
Of darkness, caused by corrupt
Hierarchy, prone to insatiate lewdness,
And abhorrent carnal desires

My dear fellow religionists,
I too share your anguish,
And interminable disdain,
When, as a Hindu, I find
My religion unnerved and
Incapacitated by archaic
Neurasthenic torpor

Come on,
Let's join together
And pray -
Our respective
Faiths and convictions
Are rejuvenated,
And Universality of Soul
Upheld

ONE CANNOT BREAK

No matter,
How powerful and intrepid,
One cannot break
The meditation of Time

Time is so immersed
In the pursuit of truth that
It seems oblivious
Even of its own existence

THEY ALL ENJOY

Literary giants
From Vedvyas and Valmiki;
To Homer and Vergil;
From Kalidas and Shakespeare;
To Tolstoy and Emerson,
They all enjoy flirting with
The poignant vibration of
Time's cry, oozing out
Of its aching heart

SILENCE OF THE MEEK

Just as a devastating explosion
Is hidden in a tiny atom,
A roaring sound of revolution
Is hidden in silence of the meek

WOULD YOU PLEASE RESCUE ME?

O solitude,
You must be hiding
Somewhere in a corner
Of my heart

Don't you see
How the cacophony
Of the world is taunting me?

Would you please
Rescue me before I get
Drawn into its hellish vortex?

O solitude,
Pray lead me to the realm
Where I can merge myself
In your solemn quietude

WHISPER OF SILENCE

Learn to be silent
Like your deep sleep

Still more silent
Is cold of death

Talk to your sleep
Converse with death

Start enjoying
The thrill of life

Life cherishes the
Whisper of silence

FIRE OF *KARMA*

If the fire of *karma* is ablaze inside you,
You will never feel tired and alone,
No matter whether you are
In solitary confinement or
In the hubbub of a bustling city
You will remain as focused
And determined as sun
Impervious to violent cosmic upheavals,
Sun never veers off its course
You will find yourself as powerful as the eternal force
That makes even the sun shine and the fire burn

YOU ARE LAW UNTO YOURSELF

O politicos,

Hearken to me

It is not serendipity that determines your success in politics

Neither does coincidence ever define your rise and fall

If you really want to be successful, follow *verbatim* what I am going to say

Politics is not only a game of expectation, but also a sleight of hands

With a weird tendency of kowtowing to magicians - unscrupulous, shrewd, sly, knavish and deceptive

Remember, if you are not a swindler at the core of your heart, don't ever enter this arena

You will achieve nothing, but despair and despondence, obloquy and opprobrium

Sadistic disposition toward trampling on peoples' head, and sinister proclivity for crushing their soul are always supposed to be extra assets in making you remarkably influential and powerful

Idiots and morons, their blood is not even worth a penny, whereas your sweat is worth a billion

Once in politics, never forget to chant 'Democracy' and 'We the People' as sacred mantras

Don't ever forget to anoint your professions and pronouncements with sleek platitudes, just to make sure that the monster inside you is never exposed

Acquisition of enormous power and inordinate wealth must be the sole objective of your political journey

You should be inherently convinced that nothing is reprehensible in the pursuit of your goal

As a politician, fighting for the cause of 'Democracy, Freedom and Liberty' you must be entitled to grand mansions, worth tens of millions of dollars

How can you correctly assess the state of your country and countrymen, including a vast majority of working people, without looking from above huge mansions and palaces?

You must not have even an iota of qualm in procuring such acquisitions

You must master the art of unleashing division and chaos in your society on the basis of, among other things, race and religion, color and creed, gender and ethnicity

You need not hesitate even to incite violence - the most potent weapon in politicians' arsenal - however, with your satanic, incendiary intentions adeptly soaked in nectarine sweetness

Cultivate within yourself the extraordinary political acumen of creating something out of nothing

As also the unabashed temerity to accuse your rivals of entire malfeasance that you commit yourself

You must not allow them even a moment to think about the country and the people; just keep them interminably entangled in legal labyrinths, involving phony investigations and concocted hoaxes

As per the need of the hour, provoke, aid and abet combustible elements that are prone to plunge the whole country into loot, arson, violence and anarchy

You have to play a consummate thespian, and pretend as though you are transcendental to all these sordid shenanigans

Go to the public, address them with a chocked voice, and shed crocodile's tears over the damage done to their lives and properties

Meantime, you should not forget to blithely segue into hurling accusations at your ideological opponents for the mayhem and inaction

You need to have a robust network of miscreants, both within and without the country

Always avoid coming into direct contact with common people

They should be treated as nothing more than trivial robots, efficiently programmed to vote for you and your organization

Learn how to take advantage out of controversies, conflicts and conspiracies

If ever questioned by some journalists about your suspected involvement, just skip

You need not deign to answer their questions

You are privileged to remain mum, based on your convenience

Make an influential conspiratorial coterie of the rich and powerful

You need not desist from enjoying carnal pleasures, no matter whoever provides them

Every moment of your life must be vibrant and aphrodisiac, because you are born to serve your people and the country

How can a person with diminished libido and declining
virility cope with the high velocity hurly burly
of politics?

Don't ever think of pleasing people; they are the
insatiate entity

As a politician, you are the one who is privileged to
wax cosmetic

Present yourself as if you are the incarnation of Jesus,
Gandhi and Mandela

Don't ever get carried away by altruistic emotions
towards insignificant worms and insects

Make it loud and clear that you are really committed to
the Constitution of the country, both in its letter
and spirit

Once in power, just shred it to pieces

You are always privileged to interpret such documents
in whatever way you want

During elections, raise enormous amount of money in
the name of people

Pour as much money as you can to buy votes for you
and your organization

If necessary, manipulate the entire state machinery in
your favor and steal votes, amidst cacophonous
din of massive misinformation campaign,
courtesy of smarmy media, unctuous
intelligentsia and groveling tech companies

It is always advisable to take a page out of books from
third world dictators such as, Hosni Mubarak,
Robert Mugabe and Nicolas Maduro, when it
comes to winning elections

Should anyone dare question your legitimacy, don't
make delay in muzzling them, threatening with

revenge and retribution through the mobilization of violent mobs and unhinged squads

Democracy, in essence, is nothing but a deceptive elitist exercise, involving the exploitation of commoners' gullibility, with grandiloquent sloganeering and sinister political grandstanding

Is there anything in the mortal world that cannot be bought with money?

Don't forget to steal as much money as you can for yourself once you are in power

Always convince yourself that even the sell-out of vital national interests is not a crime when it comes to making money and capturing power

Ethics and morality are nothing, but plaintive ululations of cowards

You can shake hands with anyone - no matter whether they are your country's friends or enemies - when it comes to shoring up your personal interests

Neither should you be hesitant in entering shadiest of the shady deals

You must not be circumscribed by elusive notions regarding your nation's integrity, sovereignty and independence

You are the citizen of the world

Never make a mistake, even inadvertently, of antagonizing alien masters

Create scores of pretensions and phony deals that help you ingratiate yourself with foreign powers

Never squander any opportunity to cash in on enemies' machinations, against your country's integrity, sovereignty and independence, no matter how vicious

Don't even denounce them, lest you should fall afoul of
formidable powerhouses, and wreck your cause
vis-a-vis domestic rivals

Always give precedence to their interests over
legitimate susceptibilities of your own country

Don't forget that they have the power and willingness
to shower you with unexpected largesse and
laud

They can go to any extent in order to enhance their
national interests

And you have to exploit their vulnerability to enrich
not only yourself, but also entire members of
your family, lackeys and toadies

Normally, people have a short memory

The mass is always pliant and malleable

You can easily obfuscate them by resorting to high
sounding rhetoric, verbose tirades, vitriolic
invectives and contorted narratives

If you don't have any idea to sell, don't worry

Just hijack your opponents' stellar plans and programs,
and produce them before the public with slight
modulation

You need not be ashamed at it, because this is what
politics is all about

In all this, you can make the most of wayward
media's and deviant intelligentsia's conscious
obsequiousness

You can easily make a common cause with them, who
seem hankering after something, material and
tangible over anything abstract and amorphous

You can easily find real soulmates in them who are
prepared even to prop up their country's enemies
in a bid to gratify their base impulses

Riding the crest of media's luscious coverage and unqualified applause, you can emerge as the formidable force to reckon with

Even so-called cultural icons with perverted psyche, arising from disproportionate wealth and synthetic fame, can be easily manipulated to boost your position

Now you don't need to be accountable to anyone

In the name of 'principled stand', you can stifle the truth

Never make a mistake of listening to the voice of your conscience

Make a habit of internalizing devious counsels of Machiavelli

Sovereignty of the people is nothing but asinine delusion

If it lies with anybody, it is with you, and only you

As far as the justice system is concerned, you need not be subservient to it

You are law unto yourself

You are above laws and the Constitution

Because you have been elected by 'sovereign people'

Even if you betray the people and your country for your personal aggrandizement, nobody can boot you out

Once you are there, you are there

You are privileged to brush aside any accusations and charges - even if they are true - as sinister conspiracy and smear campaign of the opposition

No court of law will have the temerity to indict, much less convict, you in charge of treason, corruption, malfeasance, debauchery or other wrong doings

Don't forget to stab the person in his back, once you
are elected on the strength of his endorsement
Because this is the true mantra of realpolitik, you can
forget at your own peril
Always adore peoples' verdict publicly
And trample on it while promoting your personal
interests
Freedom and liberty are your arch enemies, riding
the crest of which 'sovereign people' might
jeopardize your mission; just destroy them
Last, but not the least - even if you betray your people,
and conspire against the country, you will not
be committing any crime, provided you are
perpetuating yourself in power, and amassing
inordinate amount of wealth

*(This is a satire on how real politic works in modern day world. It is
not meant to cast aspersion on anybody or organization. It is
my earnest prayer that politics, in the comprehensive interest of
mankind, be absolved of this kind of degeneracy.)*

O YOUTHS OF CHINA, *UTTISHTHATA, JAAGRATA!*

O youths of China,
Uttishthata, Jaagrata!
You all are well aware
How the entire world is terrorized by the biological
warfare unleashed from Wuhan
Innocent people in tens of thousands have already been
killed, and millions and millions are gasping for
life
Global economy has been reduced to shambles,
Future of mankind has been subjected to chaos and
confusion, and despondence and depression
Behind all this ominous unfolding is lurking a heinous
conspiracy
Hideous visage of the ghastly demon has been unmasked
Its diabolic intent has been exposed
Who knows, all of you, the freedom-loving people of
the great ancient civilization, might one day be
inhumed *en masse* into the grave of totalitarian
monstrosity
How can you forget the decimation of Tibet and
Tibetans?
How can you forget the constant threat, hanging over
Taiwan and its people?
You might have seen with your own eyes how more
than one million people of Xinjiang have been
brutally thrown into concentration camps
How the yearning for freedom and democracy in Hong
Kong has been suppressed?

How can you forget the tragic death of Nobel laureate
Liu Xiaobo, who was long incarcerated by the
totalitarian regime
Who knows how many poets, philosophers, writers,
scholars, researchers and scientists are still
languishing in the rodent-infested, dank
basements of Chinese prisons
How can humanity forget tens of millions of people
ruthlessly killed by the 'Great Helmsman'?
Neither can the international community forget the
tragedy of Tiananmen Square where innocent
people, demanding for democracy and self
determination, were massacred in the thousands
O hapless youths,
You are neither allowed to speak your mind, nor are
you free to pursue your faith and conviction
Although you seem roaming freely,
You are not free, your are all in a state of incarceration
Your Conscience has been trampled
And your Soul crushed
The totalitarian Dragon's diabolic ambition to achieve
'tianxia' has reduced one and a half billion people
to lifeless corpses
O youths,
Come to your senses,
And realize that you are as much entitled to freedom
and liberty as are the people of Free World
You have every right to determine your own destiny
You have every right to live in freedom and liberty
Come on,
Have courage, be bold
Invoke the power of your Soul

And consign the demonic communist regime to the ash
heap of history
O great people of China, Tibet, Taiwan, Xingxiang and
Hong Kong,
Entire Free World wants to see you rise to the occasion
Wants to see you enjoy peace, prosperity and happiness
Wants to embrace you as members of its own family
Demolish the wall that separates you from the world
of freedom
Dismantle the prison that deprives you of your liberty
Destroy the ruthless juggernaut of atheist communism
that tramples on your innate yearnings for
democracy and self-determination
Make no delay in vitrifying the putrescent monolithic
structure of totalitarian regime with the molten
lava, impatiently swirling in your revolutionary
blood
O youths of China,
The world celebrates the purity and sanctitude
embedded in your aspirations
Look into the expectant eyes of the plaintive present
And don't forget
You are born to add a new chapter to the history of a
great civilization
Never has there been more propitious moment to
resuscitate your Spirit
Never has there been more opportune moment to
reinvigorate your Soul
Hato ba prapsyasi swargam
Jitwa ba bhokshase mahim,
Tasmat uttishtha …

April, 2020

108

ANTICIPATION I HARBOR

Past I reminisce
I celebrate present
When it comes to future,
Anticipation I harbor
I am silent, yet voluble
I am static, yet mobile
I seek irrelevance in relevance
I seek negativity in positivity
Status quo is the enemy of innovation,
And agitation is the root of creation
I want to take a cosmic stride
I want to travel across
Existing cultures, traditions, practices
Values, institutions, social mores,
Faiths, religions and philosophies
I dream of the day,
When stellar scientific achievements
Acquired so far in human history
Will prove completely anachronistic,
And Give way to a new horizon,
Never imagined in our wildest dream
When Krishna and Jesus
Mohammad and the Buddha
Will be rendered obsolete
Entire human beings, along with the universe
Will be bound together
By something,
Uniquely novel and exquisitely innovative
And mankind will be living in an entirely new world,

Without being encumbered by the reminiscences of
        the past,
Just like a butterfly, dancing ethereally in the air,
Leaving its ramshackle chrysalis behind

LET'S RISE TO THE OCCASION!

O my fellow beings,
We are all standing on *Kurukshetra* of Time
Look at the enemies arrayed against us
Hellbent on destroying truth, justice and righteousness,
They want to establish the empire of evil
There are some highly respected warriors, too
Such as, *Bhishma, Drona, Karna* and *Kripacharya*
But it is the injunction of *Dharma*
That they all be vanquished,
Because they are the mortal enemies
Of truth, justice and righteousness
They are here to safeguard
The diabolic ambitions of *Duryodhana,*
The ominous symbol of evil

Where there is *Duryodhana,*
There is no truth,
There is no justice,
There is no righteousness

Let's listen to the Lord's exhortation
He wants us to shed our unmanliness
And fight the war
Against evil, and its apologists
He has already blown his *panchajanya*

Come on,
Let's rise to the occasion
And defeat the forces of evil

With the invincible power of Soul
This is the moment to fight
For truth, justice and righteousness,
And establish on earth the rule of *Dharma*,
The reign of democracy, freedom and liberty

April, 2020

VIBRATION OF MY DESIRE

O my Soul,
You are the one
Who is pleased in my pleasure
You are the one
Who is tortured in my trouble
There is none except you
Whose company I really cherish
Although you seem silent,
I can hear the melody of your voice
Although you seem invisible,
I can see your beauty everywhere
Every moment of my life is
But the vibration of my desire
To be merged in your bliss

POWER OF SOUL AMERICAN

O America,
The sky will not fall,
The earth will not shatter
We won't be vanquished
As long as our spirit is alive
The enemy might be vicious, and its intent callous
But even a drop of blood American
Can destroy the regime totalitarian
For every drop of American blood
Wields the power of Soul American

April, 2020

I SALUTE YOUR EXCEPTIONAL POISE

O America,
I salute your exceptional poise,
And extraordinary composure
Even amidst the silent terror,
Pervading entire world,
You seem as steadfast as the Himalayas
That can't be intimidated by any storms,
No matter how ferocious and violent
As desperate as a mother
Who is prepared to go to any length
To save the lives of her children
I know how shocked you are
At the vicious stabbing from behind
I know how stunned you are
At the invisible enemy's diabolic intent
I am not unaware of the excruciating pain
You might be going through
But still your sense of duty and responsibility
Towards the offspring is really unparalleled

April, 2020

I WON'T FORGET YOU

O America,
I won't forget you
Even after I embark on a journey
Towards the destination unknown
Your image as the Divine,
Illuminating the destiny of mankind,
Will forever remain etched in my Soul
I won't cease to cherish your memory
Even in my afterlife, if there is any,
As a quest for freedom and liberation

A BEAUTIFUL MELODY

Out of the void
Did I appear
Onto the void
Shall I merge
Life, a beautiful melody,
Not a chanting of dirge

MY OWN STAMP

I want to put
My own stamp
On the destiny of Time
With an unflinching resolve,
I want to carve out Time's future,
Bejeweled and fragrant
I want to see Time
Fly ethereally along with
The spirit of mankind
Ever soaring high
Never looking behind

EVEN AMIDST ...

Even amidst
The cacophony of
Ominous imponderables
Appears the amber of hope

Even amidst
The raucous din of
Frightening soundbites
Appears the light of faith

Even amidst
The menacing chaos of
Sinister insinuations
Appears the power of Soul

WHY CAN'T YOU ESCAPE?

O politics,
Why can't you break the prison
Of malice, smear, vengeance,
Jealousy, revenge and retribution?
Why is your face stained with
Blood of the innocent?
Why can't you free yourself
From demons' evil ambitions?
How can you tolerate being played
Into the hands of tyrants and despots?
Aren't you meant for people
Who long for a seamless navigation
In their lives?

NEVER SHALL I VANISH

Return my body shall
To the soil, water, fire, space and air
Of what it was made
But I will forever remain with you
As your most beloved Soul
You need not mourn my departure
Nor worry about my absence
I will always be with you
Never shall I vanish

I AM THE ULTIMATE HISTORY

I embody a continuum
An eternal journey
Pursuing infinity and plenitude
I am too vast to be confined
To the narrow walls of human mind
No definition can fathom
The scope and depth of my existence
I am the ultimate history
Woven with the threads
Of past, present and future

NATURE'S INTOXICATING PANACHE

I wish
Life stopped competing
With the fleeting time,
And blithely pursued
Its own course,
Savoring enchanting vistas
Of Nature's intoxicating panache

WHEN WERE YOU BETROTHED TO ME?

O beauty of my Soul,
Please tell me
When you were betrothed to me

Although far,
I feel you are always
Close to me

Although close,
I feel you are always
Far from me

Are you mere a dream
Or an illusion?
A shadowy mirage
Or a delusion?

How long shall we live apart,
Before I from the earth depart?
Why can't we merge into one
Instead of living all alone?

O beauty of my Soul,
Please tell me
When you were betrothed to me

I TEND TO FORGET

Wallowing in sweet nostalgias,
I tend to forget my present
Sometimes

Basking in profuse laurels,
I tend to forget my truth
Sometimes

Wading in chromatic phantasies,
I tend to forget my existence
Sometimes

Groping in Stygian darkness,
I tend to forget my vision
Sometimes

Rejoicing in fragrant spring,
I tend to forget my autumn
Sometimes

MAY I KNOW WHAT IT IS!

O beauty of my imagination,
O paragon of luster and coyness,
May I know what it is -

That radiates from your eyes,
And fondles my passions!

That exudes from your glances,
And stokes my amour!

That reflects from your visage,
And agitates my senses!

That drifts from your lips,
And ignites my desires!

That flows from your aura,
And caresses my lust!

That wafts off your panache,
And inebriates my vision!

That echoes from your voice,
And vibrates my being!

That breezes from your lissomness,
And sways my restraint!

That streams from your heart,
And overpowers my will!

That embellishes your persona,
And endears you to my Self!

WHAT GOOD IS POWER?

What good is power
If it turns one into a tyrant?
What use is influence
If it fuels ambitions errant?

What good is education
If it fills one with malice and hate?
What use is wealth
If it turns one into an ogre great?

What good is beauty
If it gives one hubris and arrogance?
What use is health
If it is nothing but dismal ignorance?

LET THE PARADIGM SHIFT

O seers and sages of the global age,

Come on,

Let's seek Brahman in the sophistication of modern
world

Let's seek the Absolute in the inevitable hurly burly of
politics

Let's seek the ultimate Truth in the relentless journey
of science and technology

Let's seek the nature of reality in the cacophonous
discotheque of human relations

Let's seek Divinity in the ever mutating socio-cultural
mores and behaviors

O seers and sages of the global age,

Come on,

Let the paradigm shift

Let's stop sticking to loin clothes, tunics, beard, matted
hair and ashes

Neither must we opt for expensive vestments, exquisite
regalia and pompous insignia

Let's not allow our quest for Divinity to evaporate in
our blind adherence to petty peripherals

Let's not mistake superstition, dogmatism and
hypocrisy for simplicity, austerity and chastity

SILENCE RAINS DISASTER

Silence does not always stay silent
It could also turn extremely violent

Just like the lull before storm
Ferocious devastation might
Be germinating in its womb

Silence rains disaster,
Makes no howls
Just like a prowling cat
Makes no growls

TO SOME LIFE IS
JUST LIKE A ...

To some
Life is just like a diaphanous cloud -
Timid, timorous and teetering,
Lost somewhere in the spring sky,
Only to be dissipated by wayward winds

To some
Life is just like a dark cloud -
Dismal, dreary and dire,
Encumbered by its own distress,
Always prone to shed torrential tears

To some
Life is just like a mighty mountain -
Magnificent, massive and monumental,
Proud of its majestic existence,
Challenging formidable storms, tornadoes and
hurricanes

To some
Life is just like a solemn ocean -
Calm, composed and tranquil,
Transcendental to Nature's internecine insanity,
Often inclined to share celestial attributes with
humanity

HAPPY TO TRADE MY BLOOD

To me there is nothing worth coveting in life, save
        freedom and liberty
Just like a bird, I want to fly in the open sky, defying
        the gravity of earth
But, O Lord,
I don't beseech you to grant me these jewels for free
Accepting alms is to violate the sanctity of one's own
        Soul
Always shall I be happy to trade my blood

HOW BEAUTIFUL!

How beautiful this earth is!
I am fascinated with its color

How beautiful this life is!
I am smitten with its vigor

How beautiful this universe is!
I am mesmerized by its plurality

How beautiful this Nature is!
I am bewitched by its bounty

MAY YOU BLESS MY FELLOW BEINGS

O my poems,
The gospel of my Soul,
May you bless my fellow beings with enormous
strength and encouragement
So they can conquer the formidable mountains of their
lives
May you endow them with extraordinary boldness and
fortitude
So they can traverse the scorching deserts of their lives
May you shower upon them immeasurable patience
and perseverance
So they can cross the treacherous oceans of their lives
May you bestow upon them unimaginable courage
and vision
So they can face any challenges of their lives

O gospel of my Soul,
I can't see them cringe and cry
Even in the face of death
Pray make them realize
They are not only the children of bliss,
But also the blessed offspring of power infinite

I HAVE SOWN ITS SEED

Gospel of my Soul,
My poems carry the message of 'universality of spirit'
With utmost humility and humbleness,
I have sown its seed in the fertile soil of this great
      country, America
I don't know when, but one day for sure
It will grow into a huge *Peepul Tree*,
With its roots and branches spread across the earth
      and space
And sitting under the serene shade of this *Bodhi Plant*
Mankind will see the light of Truth, and
Humanity will find itself exalted

COMPLAINT OF A FLOWER

A nubile flower,
already upset by the impudence of wind,
shared her grievance with fiancé.
She was not happy with humans, either.
"I wonder why they just scoop us up
and place in their heart,
as if we are their personal property,"
she complained to a bumblebee,
hovering over the nymphal beauty.
"Why should you be worried about this?"
wondered bumblebee.
"Rather you should be proud that they love you,
and appreciate your beauty."
"How fair is it for them to ensconce us
in their heart even without asking for our consent?"
protested the flower.
"How can they trample on our honor and integrity,
just because they love us and appreciate our beauty?"
Bumblebee didn't speak even a word in response.
His pent up jealousy toward humans
could easily be discerned
in the echo of his enigmatic silence.

TIME'S FOURTH CHILD

Time seems not content
Only with three children
Past, Present and Future
Wants to have a fourth one, too,
Before sliding into oblivion
But is still undecided
Who should bear the fourth child for him,
Science or philosophy?

AGAIN IN THEIR LIVES

O lord,
Let the tears
Of all my fellow beings,
Whose hearts are
Bruised, injured, lacerated,
Maimed, mauled and mangled,
Stream down my cheeks,
So they won't have to cry
Again in their lives

HOW CAN I EXPRESS?

I kick you
You massage
My feet

I tread
On your body
You inspire me
To move ahead

I trample
On your persona
You show me
The direction

I violate
Your dignity
You teach me
Self-abnegation

O sidewalk,
How can I express
My gratitude
Towards your exemplary
Humility and fortitude?

I DON'T KNOW WHY MY EMOTIONS ...

O Nature,
I always admire your beauty,
But you never appreciate

O lord,
I always sing your praise,
But you never listen

O earth,
I always extol your magnanimity
But you never care

I don't know why my emotions
Don't evoke any response

O my Soul,
Pray tell me whether
I should cease to express myself
Or forget everything except you

WITH DREAMS MARIGOLD

O Deity Supreme,
Why did you create this world,
Only to confound mortals,
With dreams marigold?

O Self Supreme,
Why did you manifest
Yourself, only to enthrall innocent
Humans, in forms manifold?

O Being Supreme,
Why did you ensnare them
In the illusion of pleasure and pain,
A mystery mortals can never unfold?

NOR SHALL EVER BE

I want to read the book
That has never been written
Nor shall ever be

I want to listen to the music
That has never been composed
Nor shall ever be

I want to see the beauty
That has never been created
Nor shall ever be

DEWDROP

Dewdrop,
holding on to
the blade of grass,
evaporates
as soon as it sees
the light of sun

Just like Soul,
holding on to
our body,
becomes one with
the Being Supreme
as soon as it gets
the glimpse of Him

SHARING AGONY

Suffering
From the loneliness
Of her own dark,
Night always implores
For the company
Of light

Once spurned
By light,
Night cannot help
Crying in pain

Every morning
We see her tears,
Sharing agony
With the blades
Of grass

HEART PIERCED

All of a sudden,
The *Purusha Supreme*,
At the sight of
Reclining *Prakriti's*
Marmoreal nakedness,
Found his heart pierced
By the burning arrow
Of *Kamadeva*,
With *Rati*,
Desperate to savor
Voyeuristic pleasure,
Peeking from some corner
Of Universal Consciousness

THOU SHALT NEVER BOW

O children of Supreme Bliss,
Here is the divine injunction!
Thou shalt be bound only
By the Constitution of Spirit
Thou shalt never bow to
Any corporeal arrangements
That circumscribe thy freedom
Thou shalt live as a free Spirit
And die as an immortal Soul
Time is eternal and space infinite
Who can but thyself knit thy fate?

SPOOKY ENTANGLEMENT

A linear
Continuum of
Memories

A jagged
Journey of
Experiences

An elusive
Array of
Mirages

Life,
An iridescent spectrum
Of chromatic dreams,
With its two ends
Betrothed in
Spooky entanglement

DYSTOPIAN VORTEX OF RED

O my Soul,
Were it not for your
Divine inspiration,
I would be lost in
Dark ignorance

Nescient and benighted,
Gullible and credulous,
I would be caught in the
Dystopian vortex of Red

O my Soul,
Were it not for your
Benedictory affection,
I would be repenting
The evaporation of Conscience
And loss of my Freedom

NEVER PERTURBED

Time always seems serene,
Poised, calm and quiet
It is never perturbed by
Innumerable inflictions
It is bound to endure
It is determined to reach
The destination, no matter
How excruciating and tortuous
Its odyssey is

WHY IS MY HEART SO THIRSTY?

Why is my heart
So thirsty
To hear the melody
Of Perfection?

Where shall I find
The instrument
That can play the music
My heart is seeking
So fervently?

Why can't
Even the silent song
Of solitude
Quench the eternal thirst
Of my heart?

O my Soul,
I am wondering
If you are the same Perfection
Whose melody my heart
Is so desperate to listen to

HELP ME REMOVE

O Lord,
Help me remove
The veil
So I can see the light
Of Truth

Not in scriptures
Nor in liturgies
Can I divine the
Effulgence of truth

O Lord,
Help me remove
The veil
So I can see
the resplendence of Truth
In human Soul

MUSIC OF POISE

Abstract is my journey,
Yet resounding with abiding joy
From words to thoughts
From thoughts to wisdom
And from wisdom
All the way to my Self
An ocean of fullness and plenitude
With its exhilarating waves
Dancing to the music of poise

I WANT TO SEE YOU

O my Soul,
I want to see you

Not in preposterous exegeses
Of egotistic spiritual preachers

Not in ostentatious ceremonies
And extravagant rituals and rites

Not in expensive monuments
And architectural establishments

O my Soul,
Rather I want to see you

In the explosion of dissent
Lurking in people suppressed

In the implosion of regimes
Tyrannical, despotic and repressive

In the recognition of humans
As manifestation of the Divine

In their identification with the
Being, pervading the universe

In the advent of a new era, based
On peace, cooperation and harmony

DESTROY DEMONIC MANIA

He who has an ear
Let him hear
What the Spirit says:
"My dear fellow beings,
Wake up from your long slumber
It is not time to remain sedated
Arise and look around
You have long been deceived by those
Who claim to be your benefactors
They have engaged themselves
In suppressing your Self,
And rendering you soporific
About the pride and prestige, glory and esteem
Of your beloved country,
Obsequious to their own vested interests,
They are bent on instilling in you
Sinister illusions about yourself, your society, your
   relation with fellow beings,
As also about values and institutions you fondly cherish

"Consciously impervious to
The future of your country and your posterity,
They are trying to manipulate even your Conscience
At the most subliminal level,
Only to serve their vile interests and ambitions
Brazenly they deny you the most precious boon
The Almighty has ever bestowed upon humans -
Freedom and liberty
Apparently swayed by the spirit of evil,
They seem intent on promoting

Nefarious designs of some demonic force,
Inimical to human Conscience and human Soul

"Listen to me
They might pretend
To be your custodians, representatives,
Spokespersons, and even guardians
But essentially they are the 'Synagogue of Satans'
I have a divine message for you!
You are a free spirit, an immortal Soul
The living manifestation of the power Supreme
Subservience to any force is alien to your nature
Therefore, arise and awake!
Summon the power of your Self
And destroy this demonic mania root and branch
Enjoy freedom and liberty till the end of Time"

May, 2020

TIRELESS TRAVELER

Silent, pure and persevering,
True to the voice
Of its own conscience,
Time seems relentless
In its journey

Nobody knows
Whether or not it is
Clear about its destination
Eternity seems looking forward
To a rendezvous
With this tireless traveler

NOW IS THE TIME

Now is the time not to soothe your nerves
And render yourself inert and complacent
Rather now is the time to agitate your impulses
And turn yourself into a blazing inferno

Now is the time not to evoke mawkish devotion
And render yourself pliant and submissive
Rather now is the time to electrify your ardor
And turn yourself into an epochal volcano

O brave soldiers,
Fighting the war of Freedom
Focus yourselves
On the sword of Truth

Now is the moment to defeat forces
Bent on trampling your Conscience
Now is the time to vanquish evil
Bent on decimating your Soul

May, 2020

I HAVE YET TO SUMMON

O Lord,
Forgive me
I am not defying you
But I can't come
Without fulfilling your wish
You are the one
Who commanded me
To boil the blood of youths on earth
So they can divine
What freedom really is
And what war is really for
O Lord,
As per your wish
I have yet to summon in them
Pandavas' will and determination
So truth will triumph
And righteousness prevail

AMERICA, A BLESSED LAND

America,
A blessed land,
A glorious civilization
Nourished and nurtured
By sacred rivers -
Democracy, Human Rights, Rule of Law, Justice,
        Equality and Freedom
Pristine, pure and hallowed,
They flow down the State of Unity,
The highest mountain in the realm of Consciousness
America,
Your journey begins from individual freedom and
        liberty
And ends up in your merger with Universal Awareness
Above time, space and causality,
O Self-Luminous,
Yours is the splendor bedecking the cosmos!
Yours the majesty embellishing the creation!

BRIGHT DREAMS AND TERRIBLE NIGHTMARES

O America,
Constellation of bright dreams
Accompanied by terrible nightmares,
Showcasing corrosive insinuations and innuendoes
Now is the moment to move
Past these horrendous ordeals
Fellow Americans,
Let's pay tribute to George Floyd
By committing ourselves
To the unity of this great nation, and
By expressing our unyielding adherence
To democracy, freedom and liberty
Let's pay tribute to George Floyd
By vowing to defeat the forces,
Trying to create division among ourselves
Let's pay tribute to George Floyd
By uniting ourselves against
Violence, terror, anarchy, loot and arson
Let's pay tribute to George Floyd
By developing a sublime culture of protest,
Based on understanding, peace and harmony
Fellow Americans,
Our nation's destiny seems to have hit the inflection
        point,
Warranting a deep reflection on the reality
It was not a white kneeling on the neck of a black

It was a murderous demon blithely crushing an
      innocent
With his likes savoring the horror in broad daylight,
And cynical vultures awaiting a field day

June, 2020

DON'T EVER LET MY COUNTRY DISSOLVE

O Universal Soul,
Don't ever let my country
Dissolve in slumber!
Freedom will vanish, and
Liberty evaporate
Human conscience will be
Incarcerated, and
Soul defiled
Humans will be thrown into
Dark dungeon of dystopia, and
Humanity brutally bludgeoned
O Soul Supreme,
Don't ever let my country
Dissolve in slumber!

I AM A CHILD

Sometimes I think
I am a child,
Spoilt, pampered and mischievous
I don't give a damn
What people say about me
Occasionally I throw tantrums
I don't listen to anybody
In my paroxysm explodes
My eternal urge for something,
Pure, pristine, noble and sublime

WE ARE ALL STUDENTS

We are all students
Of the school of life
Enrolled we are
In the never ending curriculum
Every moment brings
The challenge of graduation,
Followed by reflexive impatience
To get rid of obdurate incumbrance

ABSURD PARADOXES

Consistency is not
Always consistent
Nor is coherence
Always coherent
Just like our lives
They are a mix of
Absurd paradoxes

A LUMINOUS STREAK

Just like lightning,
Life is a luminous streak
In the welkin of Time

Just like a fleeting meteor,
Evanescent and ephemeral,
Vanishing in the blink of an eye

LET THE SOARING BIRD TAKE REST

O my Soul,
O Infinite Supreme,
Why don't you allow me to be merged in your
    infinitude?
I don't want to be confined to this world of finite
It is too suffocating,
Devoid of joy and permanence
O my Soul,
Let me take refuge in your transcendence
No longer can I see myself loitering in the phantasy of
    immanence
Let the soaring bird take rest in its own nest

VIBRATE, O MY SOUL!

Vibrate, O my Soul,
Vibrate!
As much as you can, vibrate!
Let modes of Nature
Convulse, and upend the *status quo*
It is time the Self-Existent waked up,
And created a new cosmos out of Himself
Recreation, reshaping and reordering
Of the cosmos seems to be long overdue
Let innumerable supernovas explode,
And a new set of stars, planets and galaxies emerge

Vibrate, O my Soul,
Vibrate!
As much as you can, vibrate!
Let there be massive black holes
To devour untruth and injustice,
Plaguing the divine order,
Based on your immanence
Let your sovereignty be established
So humans and humanity
Get bestowed with
Enormous love and compassion,
Power and strength

WHY SHOULD I BE GRATUITOUS?

O my Soul,
Pray help me
Dedicate this body of mine,
Subject to decay and death,
To some lofty cause
Why should I be gratuitous
As to yield to the Grim Reaper,
Without anything substantial
In return?

WHAT A BIZARRE ANOMALY!

What a bizarre anomaly!
Law breakers are rewarded,
And law abiding citizens punished
What a grotesque irony!
Sacred documents are denounced
And profane ravings celebrated
What is it that is constantly
Gnawing at our conscience?
And what is it that is ceaselessly
Corroding our judgment?
No wonder,
Agamemnons commit excesses
And Achilleses suffer

August, 2020

COULD YOU LEARN SOMETHING?

O death,
Why is your quietude
So different from that of solitude?
Never do the mortals
Long for your cuddle
Even gods don't want
To listen to your fiddle
Could you learn something from solitude?
So you might be endearing to multitude
O death,
Why is your tranquillity so dreadful
Whereas that of solitude is
Solemn, sublime and blissful?

LET US PURSUE

Where is the beauty of our Being?
Where is the bliss of our Self?
Where is the truth of our existence?
Let us pursue the underlying reality
With strong resolve and persistence

WHERE IS TRUTH, BEAUTY AND BLISS?

What am I supposed to write about?

Sun, moon, stars, galaxies, supernovas, quasars and nebulae?

Oceans, mountains, deserts, prairies, plains and plateaus?

After all, it is only a matter of time

The day will come when they will all disappear

In the unfathomable darkness of time

Maybe to give way to some mesmerizing phenomena

And outlandish eruptions,

Hitherto unknown even to science, philosophy and religion,

Let alone poor human beings, supposedly organic tiny bubbles, fleeting, transient and ephemeral

Am I supposed to write about politics, economy, ecology, and environment?

Am I supposed to write about kings, emperors, presidents, empires, regimes and administrations?

Am I supposed to write about satraps, vassals, dictators, despots, tyrants and conquerors?

Am I supposed to write about the sleazy, sordid, corrupt and debauched conduct and behaviors of politicians?

Or about the pernicious, corrosive, fluid and mercurial relationship among themselves?

Am I supposed to write about sex, nudity, obscenity, prostitution, promiscuity, and host of perversions relating to sexual lives?

Am I supposed to write about race, religion, caste, creed, color, ethnicity and origin?

Am I supposed to write about conflicts, tensions, skirmishes, battles and wars?

Am I supposed to write about rebellions, revolts, treason and sedition?

As a bard, constantly engaged in seeking truth, I find myself always confused

Where does the truth really lie?

What is beauty, and what is bliss?

Is philosophy, religion and science the answer?

Or there is something else beyond them, too?

Is it possible to remove the golden leaf and have a glimpse of truth, by getting embroiled in ever flowing, transient phenomena of this world of appearance?

Or I need to go deep into the nature of reality?

O my Soul,

Pray enlighten me

Where is truth, beauty and bliss?

THEY ARE ALL DIVINE VIBRATION

Ishabasyamidam sarbam …
Entire cosmos is wrapped up in you
There is nothing
That is not enveloped by your persona
Both immanent and transcendent
At the same time,
You are everything and everything is you
I find you in everything,
From sub-atomic particle to the vast cosmos
I can discern both relativity and quantum
In the esoteric dance of *Nataraja*
O lord,
You are everything -
Lyrics, music, notes, instruments, singer, and even
        audience and ambiance
Truly you are *Brahman*,
The reality underlying the apparent world
Each and everything in this universe,
Whether animate or inanimate
Breathes your life
O lord,
With utmost humbleness, I must sincerely admit
To me each and every object is equally divine
Each and every life is equally honorable
Each and every color is equally beautiful
Each and every sound is equally melodious
They are all divine vibration of the Supreme,
Embowering the cosmos

I DO CELEBRATE THE UNITY

Different colors
Different sizes, and
Different forms

Different proportions
Different symmetries, and
Different balances

Different creeds
Different races, and
Different religions

Different faiths
Different convictions, and
Different dispositions

Different ethnicities
Different origins, and
Different backgrounds

Colorful diversity
I do admire indeed
Even more than that
I do celebrate the unity
Lurking behind

August, 2020

LIGHT OF FREEDOM
AND DIVINITY

Poetry writhing in agony
Philosophy stupefied
Religion groping in darkness
Arts cringing with fear
Innocents brutally murdered
Even women and children not spared
Freedom and liberty suffering asphyxiation
Red-faced nights seething at arsonists' atrocities
White-faced days ashamed at helplessness
Where is law?
And where is order?
O my beloved America,
Why does the ambience seem so ominous?
Why is our conscience so numb?
Black or white, red or brown
Each color has their own beauty,
Drawn from the Being of Nature
Just as seven colors coalesce
To enhance the luminosity of sun,
In the multiplicity of hues
Human existence brightens
And in their plurality
Blossoms human ingenuity
Blood of the innocent
Does not add to their aroma
Rather it robs them
Of their magnificent fragrance
No matter what race or color
Each human is divine unto himself

Carved in the image of the Almighty
America, rest assured
Never shall your greatness be diminished
By some deviants' unscrupulousness
Forces of doom and darkness
Seem hurtling themselves
Toward the footnotes of history
An exciting chapter of freedom
and divinity is about to dawn

August, 2020

WHO IS NOT TOUCHED?

Who is not touched
By the sublime beauty of a woman,
With her slender fingers,
Stroking the hair of a man,
Comfortably laying his head on her lap,
And the ambience perfumed
By the fragrance of love,
Overflowing the rendezvous
Of inebriated eyes?

RADIANT IS YOUR REALM

Just like sun,
You illuminate the universe of mankind
Radiant is your realm
With transcendental harmony and happiness
Were it not for you
This world would be nothing
But death, doom and darkness
O America,
The most cherished philosophy of freedom
You represent the cosmic energy
Ensuing from the Being Supreme
You represent the undying spirit
Flowing from the Deity Supreme
You manifest yourself in equality and justice
You manifest yourself in peace and prosperity
You manifest yourself in power and strength
You manifest yourself in love and compassion
O America,
The most cherished philosophy of liberty
May you bless entire mankind with eternal hope and
     optimism
May you bless humanity with unceasing calm and
     tranquility

GITA'S IMMORTAL MESSAGE TO THE YOUTH OF WORLD

You were never born
Nor will you ever die
It is not that
You were not in the past
Nor will you ever cease to be
You are not subject to
Change, decay and death
You are eternal and infinite
There is nothing
That can destroy you
You are a free spirit,
An immortal Soul
You are the Self Supreme unto yourself
Tattwamasi!
O youths of the world,
Arise and awake!
With the invincible weapon of
Nishkama Karmayoga
Decimate the forces,
Bent on crushing your Self,
And trampling on your conscience
Without being a bit daunted
Stand up to forces
That are prone to assault
Truth and righteousness
Don't ever waver

When it comes to fighting
For freedom and liberty,
The ultimate goal and ideal
Of each mortal on earth

DO I CHERISH YOU

I cherish you, my dear
Always, always, always
Do I cherish you

In the twinkling of stars
In the light of moon
Do I cherish you, my dear
Always, always, always

In everything,
Solemn and sublime,
Noble and calm
Do I cherish you, my dear
Always, always, always

In my mind and conscience
In my heart and soul
Do I cherish you, my dear
Always, always, always

In the rhythm and notes of life
In the music and beauty of existence
Do I cherish you, my dear
Always, always, always

NO MATTER HOW ...

No matter
How gorgeous, majestic and elegant,
You never enter a palace
With the same reverence, humility and submissiveness
That your heart gets imbued with
While entering a temple,
No matter
How dilapidated and ramshackle

YOU HAVE ENVELOPED

Those who are thirsty
See you in water
Those who are hungry
See you in food
Those who are active
See you in action
Those who are miserable
See you in happiness
Those who are destitute
See you in prosperity
O lord, my Soul,
Really, you have enveloped
Every aspect of human existence!

I AM INFATUATED

I am infatuated with my Self
I am in love with my Self
I am smitten with my Self
I look at my Self
I taste my Self
I smell my Self
I touch my Self
I hear my Self
Beyond my Self
There is nothing worth
seeing, tasting, smelling, touching and hearing
There is nothing worth doting on

YOU ARE THE MIGHTIEST WARRIOR

O poet,
You are the mightiest warrior
Is there any weapon on earth
That can match your words?
You fight with passion and empathy,
Emotion and sympathy
Embedded in your Being are
Tears and smiles, ecstasy and agony
With love you can melt stones
With words of courage and boldness,
Tenderest of hearts you can freeze
You can see all past, present and future
Nothing is beyond your grasp
Mere at your frowning mighty empires crumble
Since your words come out of invincible Soul

AN UNASSUMING BARD

"Eons ago
I had written some poem
Not to spread my name and fame
But to invoke the Soul Supreme
And to fulfill my cherished dream"

Thus spake an unassuming bard
Who would always hate canard
About the country
And people he loved
With the spirit of a true sentry
Entire mankind often he served

MAY I SAVOR THE EXHILARATION

O my Soul,
May I retain
The honor and privilege
Of freely walking the streets
With utmost humility of humble ants,
Without being noticed by spying eyes
Of society, and the powers that be
May I savor the exhilaration
Of breathing fresh air,
Unpolluted by the miasma
Of recognition and investiture
O my Soul,
I don't want to see you obscured
By false ego and arrogance
They tend to stoke

HAVEN OF BEGGARS

O my Soul,
Let not my country turn
Into a haven of beggars,
With weary, expectant eyes
Waiting in line for hours
Only to get a morsel of food
Let not my country turn
Into a ragtag sanctuary
Where people kill precious
Moments of their lives
Yearning for measly alms
O my Soul,
I can't see my beloved country
Precipitating towards dystopian fantasy
Let this land of the brave
Be flooded with milk an honey,
Bread and butter,
Cereals, grains and legumes,
Fruits and vegetables
Let this home of the free
Be inundated
With poultry and sea foods,
Red meat and fowls
Let the lands of this country be fertile and productive
Let our rivers, streams and lakes be clean and pellucid
Let our environment be free from pollution
Let our plains, prairies, plateaus, deserts, hills and
      mountains silently continue to sing the immortal
      song of unity,
Underlying the empirical existence

Let varieties of industries flourish
Let us have as many jobs as will be needed for growing
      population
Let sons and daughters of my country be highly
      motivated to work,
And live a life with full dignity and honor
With unceasing enthusiasm, vigor and optimism,
Let them enjoy the splendor of life with meaning,
      purpose and goal
Let them be sober, cultured and noble,
With abiding commitment to peace, harmony,
      cooperation and coexistence
Let them be inherently inclined towards seeking unity
      in diversity
O my Soul,
Over and above,
Let them fathom the true essence of freedom and
      liberty,
And cultivate within themselves inveterate penchant
      for protecting and preserving them
With exceptional courage and a missionary zeal,
Let them share these values with entire mankind
Let them live on earth,
Not as a wretched object of condescension,
But as a free spirit and an immortal Soul

August, 2020

O BRAVE SOLDIERS ...

O brave soldiers
Of freedom and liberty,
Democracy and rule of law,
Beleaguered mankind
Has pinned great hope on you
No matter,
How arduous and tortuous your journey,
You are destined to prevail
Odds are exceptionally heavy
Challenges are really formidable
Demonic juggernauts
Are bent on crushing you,
With proxies worldwide
Blithely dancing to their morbid tune
But the purity of your mission,
And the cosmic power of your Soul
Have rendered you invincible

August, 2020

NOCTURNAL PREDATOR

O nocturnal predator,
Why do you sneak
Into my room from the window
At midnight?
As soon as you enter my room,
You start caressing me
With your mesmerizing touch,
And fondling me
With your marmoreal body,
Vibrating with passion and amour
I can't but start melting

Immersed in the smoochy ambience,
Streaming from your lissome beauty,
And sublime fragrance,
I get completely lost in titillating transports,
Silently once you whisper in my ear
Only to vent your smoldering lust

When I come to my senses
I find you already hidden in the Western horizon,
Amidst the reddish glow of the morning
Maybe you don't want your secret
Revealed to the Sun

LET ME VANISH

Just as the diaphanous
Cloud vanishes into the blue sky,
O my Soul,
Let me vanish in your majesty
Just as the salt is embedded
In the water of ocean
O my Soul,
Let me be embedded in your grandeur
Just as the fragrance is hidden
In the beauty of a flower
O my Soul,
Let me be hidden in your splendor

IS THERE ANOTHER WORLD BEYOND?

"Is there another world beyond the horizon?" I asked
my Soul.

"Yes, there is," he said.

"How is it?" I wondered.

"It is unimaginably beautiful and gorgeous", he replied.

"Would you please escort me to that world?" I implored.

"Sure," he condescended. "But on one condition."

"What is it?" I demanded.

"Just like a wriggly caterpillar, solely on the strength
of its will and determination, turns itself into
a superbly exquisite art of Nature, you need to
harbor an intense passion for metamorphosis,
and identify yourself with me," he assured.

O IMMORTAL HEROES
OF AMERICA!

O soldiers of this great country
O valiant warriors of freedom and liberty
Humanity is forever indebted to you
Your blood is the sacred symbol of bravery,
With a glorious legacy of valor and chivalry
Just because of you,
Not only America and Americans are safe,
The whole world feels ensconced
In your abiding commitment
To fighting tyranny and injustice
Whether it be in Vietnam
Or in the Korean War,
Or in Iraq and Afghanistan,
Or other war-torn countries of Europe and Africa,
Your exemplary prowess, and devotion to duty
With unparalleled military acumen,
Was glaringly displayed
You were the ones
Who had decisively changed
The course of human history
During the two Great Wars
Of the twentieth century,
By trouncing the brutal forces,
Determined to crush truth and justice
Apparently afraid of your invincible power,
Cold War enemies dissolved into submission,
With the evil empire itself vanishing
In the terribly phantasmal socialist smoke,
Surrounding the dictatorship of proletariats

O brave guarantors of freedom and liberty,
How can human civilization forget your illustrious
            feats?
Just like Arjuna, the invincible hero of the *Mahabharata*,
You have inspired mankind to reaffirm
Its commitment to truth, justice and righteousness,
By destroying dreaded monsters like Bin Laden,
Zarqabi, Al Baghdadi and Sulaimani
O brave sons of this great country,
Were it not for you,
We would still be groping in the dark
For a tiny shred of light
Stakes have never been higher
Redoubtable enemies of freedom and liberty
Are spreading their totalitarian tentacles
As though they are going to devour the entire world
Nescient as they are,
Some gullible elements
Seem reveling in the macabre tune
Of their conspiratorial benediction,
And portraying our existence as something
Unceremonious, profane, depraved and callous
Consigning our sacred values and institutions
To the trash can of cancel culture,
They seem determined to turn this land of the free
Into a safe haven of beggars and mendicants,
With their ragtag encampments strewn
Across the destiny of this home of the brave
But how long the source of evil will sustain itself?
However giant, colossal and powerful,
Supernova cannot stop itself from exploding

O valiant heroes of America,
Under your valorous steadfastness,
We want to see freedom and liberty
Spread across the earth and space,
With the enemies of
Human conscience and human Soul;
Peace, prosperity and harmony,
Reduced to insignificant footnotes of history

O immortal heroes of America,
May the undying spirit
Of Star Spangled Banner
Always inspire you to uphold
The sanctity of human existence!

August, 2020

LET NOT MY THIRST
BE QUENCHED!

O my Soul,
Let not my thirst for writing
Be ever quenched
Let the Mississippi and the Amazon
Of my thoughts
Continue to flow forever
Let them nurture and nourish
The ecosystem
Of human imagination and ingenuity
May humans and humanity
Be forever blessed
With serene tranquility, and solemn calm
Streaming from the Mississippi and the Amazon
Of my thoughts

I AM NOT INTERESTED

I am not interested
In pursuing a beaten track
History to me is only an ignition
That sparks imagination and ingenuity
In the momentous outpourings of
Great thinkers and writers,
From Veda Vyasa, Homer and Virgil
To Shankaracharya, Emerson and Krishnamurti
I find the message of motion and dynamism
I don't see them as symbols of stagnation
They always inspire me
To dive into the world of the unknown
So I can find something,
New, and even strange and outlandish,
Quite different from
What was discovered in the past
Quest for the new and the unknown
Gives purpose and meaning to life

A PRAYER

You're my journey,
Destination you are
You're my strength,
Resolution you are
O my Soul,
Never in life, nor in death
Shall I waver from this faith

HOW BEAUTIFUL A COEXISTENCE!

Krishna, Buddha, Mahavir,
Socrates, Jesus and Gandhi
Ebullient faces of the same Soul
Residing in every human being,
Including myself, and the tiny bees,
That not only sweeten our existence,
But also give life to every creature on earth,
By sustaining the ecology of our planet
What an amazing interconnectedness!
How beautiful a coexistence!
Even beyond the comprehension
Of mythological Gods and deities,
Constantly warring for power and influence,
Fleeting, ephemeral and transient

POOR ROBOTS!

How unfortunate!
These robots cannot read
The poignant poetry
Of broken hearts!
They are mere machines,
As if programmed only to listen
To the music of nether world
Under the command
Of some sly, manipulative master,
Devoid of human empathy,
And human Soul,
They seem reveling
In the chaos and cacophony
Of suffering, torture and agony
Poor robots,
How can they distinguish
What is truth and what is untruth!

September, 2020

I MIGHT SOUND WEIRD

I might sound weird to many
Even in the age of Artificial Intelligence
I play the song of Soul,
And implore the world to revel
In the melody of Self
With passion intense do I delve
Into the esoteric realm of Brahman,
And entreat fellow beings to embark
Upon a journey towards their own Being
When science is engaged
In the relentless quest for a unified theory
That can describe our existence,
I am expounding the primacy of Universal Consciousness,
As the underlying reality,
Behind the beginning and the end of the cosmos
To me my poems are the gospel of my Soul,
And their pronouncements
Vibration of the Spirit Supreme

'YEAST OF THE PHARISEES'

"There is nothing covered
That will not be revealed,
Or hidden
That will not be known"
Dear countrymen,
Beware of the 'unseen graves'!
'Yeast of the Pharisees'
Might destroy values, institutions,
And sacred documents,
Foundational pillars
Of the Shining City on a Hill
It might desecrate
The purity, virtue and sanctity
Of our beloved motherland
The Paragon of freedom and liberty
Might be betrayed
At the hands of 'Hypocrites',
Prone to ingratiate themselves
With totalitarian Herod
Dear fellow Americans,
Let's rise to the occasion,
And unmask the forces,
Determined to vanquish
Truth and righteousness
It is time we reinvigorated within ourselves
The highest spirit of America,
And swore our undying allegiance
To the Star Spangled Banner!

September, 2020

205

REDUCED TO AN INANIMATE CHARIOT

O my Soul,
Why does my mind seem meandering,
And intellect dithering?
My senses seem oscillating
Between ecstasy and agony
Why does my existence appear lachrymose?
As if I am drowned in the whirlpool of debilitating
emotions
Why am I reduced to an inanimate chariot
Driven by wayward horses,
With a nescient charioteer
Holding agitated reins?
What is it that constantly deters me
From identifying myself
With the real master of the chariot,
Ebulliently calm, quiet and tranquil?

CONTINUED TO FLOW

I was rummaging in the earth
In the space
And even in the vast universe
'What are you looking for?'
Asked my Soul
Impudently indifferent to his question,
Was I continuing with my fervent quest
"Here you go", with an amorous streak in his nascent
        smile, he handed me my shadow
Exulted at his affectionate gesture,
I expressed my deep gratitude,
And continued to flow like a *nirmal* river,
Embracing my shadow's undulating waves

MARBLES OF WORDS

I am a child
I enjoy playing with marbles
Shiny and colorful marbles of words
Just like Legos,
With these marbles
I make different kinds of toys and decorative items
Using the magic glue of emotion, reason and rationality
I make beautiful flowers, trees, animals, cars, airplanes,
    rockets, and many more
Even human beings and the globe
What is interesting is
In humans, I instill the sense of humanity with divine
    fragrance,
And in the globe, universal consciousness
With the same marbles I create
The rhythm and notes of *Maya*'s celestial music
Even Supreme *Purusha* cannot resist the temptation of
    listening to its melody

I MAY NOT HAVE TO ...

O my Soul,
May I see something,
After seeing which
I may not have to see anything?
May I speak something,
After speaking which
I may not have to speak anything?
May I hear something,
After hearing which
I may not have to hear anything?
May I smell something,
After smelling which
I may not have to smell anything?
May I feel something,
After feeling which
I may not have to feel anything?

DON'T WORRY

"Today I sorely feel like crying",
Said my pen.
"Why?" I asked.
"I see the future of mankind sliding towards a
dystopian abyss", said he.
As I was about to paint my copy lachrymose in
deference to my pen's poignance,
My Soul suddenly interjected,
"Don't worry, truth will certainly triumph, and
mankind will be blessed with redemption."

September, 2020

THE LANGUAGE OF LIFE

The language of life is too complex for those
Who don't comprehend the words of existence
Who don't know the basic grammar of relationship
Who don't understand the syntax of human emotions
Who don't appreciate the simile of amour
And who don't reckon the metaphor of impulses

THE LABYRINTH
OF ILLUSION

I am always in search of something
But I don't know what it is
I am always desperate to reach somewhere
But I don't know where it is
I am always fervently seeking someone
But I don't know who it is
O my Soul,
Could you please tell me?
Where the end of my quest is!
Or I am forever destined to be lost
In the labyrinth of illusion!

FULL OF DARK PARADOXES

A rotten torso lying on the filth
Delectable feast of vultures and hyenas
Forced to endure their gruesome mauling
Life, a journey replete with cruelties

The mechanized body of a prostitute
Sadistic pleasure of insatiate psychos
Forced to endure thousands of rapes
Life, a continuum of disgusting agony

The excruciating pain of a cancer patient
Victim of relatives' agonizing indifference
Forced to endure the entire torture of earth
Life, a destiny of crumbled icicles

The unfathomable optimism of an *arhant*
Exulted moments of enlightened odyssey
Forced to celebrate inexplicable future
Life, the light full of dark paradoxes

April, 2006

ETERNAL ROAR OF
HUMAN SOUL

I don't believe in Time
I don't believe in Space
They are mere illusions
They try to constrain me
They try to incarcerate me

I am above both Time and Space
I am not even the universe
I am the one who created it
Neither have I any beginning
Nor do I have any end

I don't belong to any religion
I don't believe in any faith
I am both religion and faith unto myself
Never do I need mercy of any god
Both moksha and nirvana pursue me

FROWN

The night wrapped
in its own darkness, and
the day blazing with light,
both try to frown upon me

A LIFE INFURIATED

A life
Infuriated
At its
Own vacuity
Longs
To be cherished
Both
By saints and Satans,
So
It can
Bask in its
Sham eternity

BLOODTHIRSTY SPECTER

An ambience reverberating
With scornful guffaw of grave,
Dug millions of years ago

The corpse has disappeared
People believe
It has turned into some atheistic entity,
And is practicing an austere penance
In a monolithic civilizational cave

It is trying to propitiate
Its warring past
By invoking sanguinary escapades
Of maniacal monarchs and satraps
To achieve the most coveted goal –
To be established as *chakravarti samrat*
Once its wish is granted
It also seems determined
To perform a*shwamedha yajna,*
And fill massive graves with
Human beings' intrinsic yearning
For freedom and liberty

The world will then suffer
The gruesome megalomania
Of a bloodthirsty specter,
Disguising itself as a benign Dragon

Only the future can reveal
Whether or not
It is only a morbid fantasy
Of a spirit, evil and demoniac

March, 2006

CHERISHING MY LOVE

The sun has already disappeared
There is no more light on earth
The moon is still unborn

I want to forget the moments
When you had kissed my fingers
Even a furtive glance of mine
Would shower blush on your face

Along with the arrival of winter
Vibrant streams have begun to dry up
Ships are not bothered for having
Failed to leave any trace behind

I can't count on my own future
It might play into the whims of destiny
World, too, might suffer amnesia
But you still seem cherishing my love

March, 2006

AMOROUS TOUCH

When I am teased by
The smirks of my tears
I try to conceal myself
Behind the veil of wind

Wind, as it is impetuous,
Wants me to join its
Vivacity, emblazoned with the
Caresses of many an existence

Oblivious of the past, and
Impervious to the future,
The wind is always in
Quest of a new destination

Wind's flirtation with
The beauty of Nature
Is something, human
Senses always cherish

The melody flowing
From the whisper of wind
Gives my heart
An amorous touch

ALTER EGO OF
CRUEL DESTINY

Romeo and Juliet
Heer and Ranjha
Laila and Majnu
Tender milestones of love,
Exuding eternal fragrance

Love,
A subtle sensation,
A psychedelic peregrination
And sometimes,
An aesthetic attempt at
Seeking one's own being

Love is both
Relative and absolute
Love is hate, and
Hate love,
An enigmatic paradox

Shah Jahan,
Out of profound love
Towards his other half, Mumtaz,
Built Taj Mahal,
One of the most wonderful creations
In human history

The Mughal emperor ordered
Architects' hands and fingers
Chopped off,

Hideous metamorphosis of love

Incarcerated both by his successor
And cruel destiny,
The monarch
Could not even touch
The beauty of the monument
He built in fond memory of his wife

It was only after his death,
That he was allowed to caress his beloved,
For he was entombed
Alongside his own heart

Love sometimes
Enjoys playing alter ego
Of cruel destiny

November, 2005

TEARS AND LONELINESS

Let not tears and loneliness
Stifle your joy and happiness
Life is too short to be spent
In sheer remorse and lament

LET NOT YOUR
LIFE DISSOLVE

Let not your life
Dissolve into tears!

Look at the vines
How they find themselves
Exulted by developing courtship
With trees and their branches!

Let not your life
Dissolve into loneliness!

Look at the silence
How it finds itself poised
By forming liaison with
Solitude!

HOLD BACK JUST
FOR A MOMENT

Solitary advocate of freedom and liberty,
True symbol of truth and righteousness,
O America,
Hold back, just for a moment,
Your dazzling resplendence
And blinding effulgence,
Flowing from your undying commitment
To the Divine Spirit,
Inherent in every individual,
So I can behold
Your majesty, grandeur and grace,
And recognize my own Self
In your Soul Supreme!

DIVINELY INVINCIBLE

O my Soul,
Let me turn
Your purity, calm and sacredness
Into indomitable will, determination,
Power and strength,
So I may emerge as a force,
Divinely invincible,
Never giving in
To untruth, injustice,
And unrighteousness!

A NEW PERSPECTIVE

"I don't even know
How this 11-member organization
Originated

"I have no idea
Where this lethal organization
Is registered

"However,
It seems exceptionally
Agile and robust

"Nobody knows
For sure, who are
Financing this organization

"Whoever they might be,
They must be the loyal
Agents of evil

"Maybe some
Extra territorial elements
Are also involved

"How can it be
So sustainable without
The support of great powers?

"Look what they have done!
Just like a raging storm
Ravaging innocent villages

"Everything crushed
To the ground, not even hopes
And aspirations spared

"How cruel and brutal!
I can't describe
I can just feel the pain

"Promising and beautiful
Flowers ruthlessly
Nipped in the bud

"Aged, incapacitated
And helpless shrubs, plants
And trees burnt alive

"Young, energetic,
Benevolent, handsome
And fragrant plants cruelly hacked

"Ingenuity, endeavor,
Innovation, enthusiasm
And creation bludgeoned

"Peace and harmony,
Order and stability
Burnt in broad daylight

"Unprecedented reign
Of terror unleashed
With absolute impunity

"Widespread cheering
And incendiary applause,
Further fueling the flame

"Entire land engulfed
In dark clouds of smoke, raging
From hellish conflagration"

"What is it
That you are so seriously
Ruminating on?" asked my Soul

"It is all about the
Devastation, and subsequent misery,
Caused by some brutal elements," I replied

"Do you have any idea,
Who they really are?"
He questioned

"I am
Not sure," I said

"Listen," continued my Soul.

"They are none other
Than the set of your own
Sensory organs

"It is an amorphous organization
Of eleven members, registered nowhere
But in your own body

"They comprise of
Five *Jnyanendriyas*, five
Karmendriyas plus your own mind

"These are the sense
Organs that express themselves
In different ways

"Such as, rage, hatred, vengeance,
Lie, deception, sabotage, conspiracy,
Loot, violence, arson and anarchy

"If trained and restrained,
They prove immensely
Great and beneficial

"If not, they might
Cause great harm,
And even complete destruction

"You have to understand
The whole phenomenon
In this way

"The land you are
Referring to is
Your own body

"The plants, shrubs,
Flowers and trees all
Represent your potentials

"Whatever you are musing on
Are nothing but different
Dimensions of your consciousness

"Under the enigmatic spell of *Maya*
You tend to take them for something
Real, tangible and manifest

"The devastation you
Were ruminating on is the
Destruction of your existence as a human

"Certainly, such an
Apocalypse cannot be caused
Without the support of outside forces

"They tend to lure
You into the hell by dangling
Savory objects before you

"They are the enemies
Who incite your senses
To wreak havoc in your world

"They have their own
Interest in using your
Senses as their tools

"Some elements inside
Your own body fervently
Cherish their benediction

"And your senses, nescient as
They are, tend to succumb
To their devious machinations

"You get swayed by ignorance,
Coupled with such enticement, both from
Within and without

"Once the decline sets in,
It will be very difficult to stop it
From further precipitating

"No doubt, it will exhilarate
Both miscreants within yourself
And the enemies without

"But in due course of time
Your dignity and honor
Will start corroding

"Your existence
As a sovereign entity
Will be lost

"You will relegate yourself
To a meek pawn at the hands of
Enemies' proteges

"And that will be the
Point of total destruction when
You lose your free will and conscience

"This is how your identification with
Me as a free Spirit and an immortal Soul
Will forever be doomed"

Thus
Following the discourse
Of my Soul,
Dawned on me
A new perspective
About my body, myself,
My present and my future

October, 2020

WOE TO THE REGIMES!

Woe to the regimes
Where, instead of water,
Tears of pain and misery of the hapless
Flow in their rivers

Woe to the regimes
Where mountain peaks,
Instead of blushing at the flirtation of nascent sun,
Appear to be stained with blood of the innocent

Woe to the regimes
Where winds,
Instead of whispering beautiful melody,
Echo the gasping of asphyxiated masses

Woe to the regimes
Where lives,
Instead of dancing to the tune of Spring,
Wither in the emaciation of etiolated Autumn

ETERNAL URGE OF HUMAN EXISTENCE

O enemies of freedom and liberty,
The day will come
When you will find yourself
Reduced to the footnotes of history
You will find yourself crushed
Under the glowing chapters,
Singing praise of valiant heroes
Whose love for the country and countrymen
Will forever continue to ignite in every heart
The blazing fire of vibrant patriotism
Whose unyielding steadfastness
Will evermore inspire the world as a metaphor
Of mighty mountains,
Standing against violent storms and devastating
hurricanes
Whose pronouncements
Will vibrate the Soul and Conscience
Of entire humans and humanity
And whose sacrifice will consecrate freedom and
liberty
Into eternal urge of human existence

October, 2020

RELATION WITH
OUR SHADOW

What is our relation
With our shadow?
Why does it seem so infatuated with us,
And doesn't leave us
Even for a moment?
If it is its love toward us,
Does it accompany us even after our death?
If so,
How does it look like
When our body is reduced to ashes,
And *prana* merged into space?

A MOMENT WITH FEAR

O fear,
Have you ever
Feared yourself?

O fear,
Who made you
So fearsome?

O fear,
Have you ever had
Courtship with love?

O fear,
Why is your realm
So dark?

O fear,
Why do you cherish
Our destruction?

O fear,
How big is your
Empire?

O fear,
When were you
First born?

O fear,
Why can't you touch
Sun, moon and stars?

O fear,
Why are you so
Infatuated with us?

O fear, I prefer
To be jilted than to be in
Love with you

O fear, why
Are you so jealous
Of my calm?

O fear, why
Do you foray into
My poise?

A MOMENT WITH MY TEARS

Oceans are
Poignant collection
Of my tears

I wish
My tears could
Speak

Gap between
Tears and smiles
Worlds apart

How deep is
The source of
Our tears?

Why can't our
Shadows shed tears
Over our misery?

When shall
We be able to hear
The cry of tears?

O my tears,
What is the source
Of your agony?

O my tears,
Tell me how I can

Share your pain!

O my tears,
When will your source
Dry up?

O my tears,
Please stop streaming,
I cannot see you

Were it not for
My tears, I'd have
Frozen in agony

O my tears,
Why are you so
Poignant?

Playing into hands
Of tears and smiles
Oscillating pendulum

A MOMENT WITH TIME

O time,
Would you please stop
For a moment?

O time,
Are we mere puppet
At your hands?

O time,
Do you also have
An end?

O time,
Where does your
Power come from?

O time,
How did you learn
To be so patient?

O time,
Would you share your
Patience with me?

O time,
How mysterious
Your silence is!

Time's eternal
Infatuation with silence
Evokes passions

When I die
Time comes to an end
Sounds puzzling?

THOU ART THE ONE

O my Soul,
Thou art the one
Under whose command
Gleefully blows the wind
With its melody trailing behind

O my Soul,
Thou art the one
Under whose command
Vibrantly flows the river
Forgetting its past forever

O my Soul,
Thou art the one
Under whose command
Cheerfully shine sun and moon
Bestowing upon us precious boon

AESTHETIC ECHO

The West
Is not a tango dance
Between
Soda and pizza,
Virility and beauty,
Testosterone and estrogen
Rather,
It
Is an aesthetic echo
Of Unity,
Underscoring
The nature of reality

HARBINGER OF ARMAGEDDON

Papyri have begun to decay and decompose,
With the divine message evaporating
As if it were scribbled on them
With the ink of camphor
Books and newspapers seem reduced
To mere biodegradable objects,
Reeking of intolerable putrescence,
Apparently with their Soul defiled
By blood-stained footsteps
Of dastardly dragon and brutal bear
Even our own scientific innovations,
Painstakingly reared and nurtured by Freedom
With motherly affection,
Seem to have turned matricidal
O my Soul,
What has gone amiss!
Is it mere an episodic aberration,
Or the ominous harbinger of Armageddon?

October, 2020

I AM THE SOURCE

I am the source
of rivers that
stir up your blood

Rocks and boulders
of your body hanker
for my electric touch

My intrusion into
your landscape gives you
transports of trance

The more you move,
the more you remain
supine and motionless

This is the world
that we want to
change into stone

JOY OF A BIG FAMILY

I am savoring the joy of a big family
America, you are the nucleus of this institution
Everyone in this world is the member of my own family
I share weal and woes with them
I don't care what race, religion, creed, color, ethnicity
        and origin they belong to
I don't care whether they are rich or poor
I don't even care about their educational status
After all they are all my own brothers and sisters
When they go to the temple, I go with them and
        meditate on Brahman
When they go to the church, I go with them and pray
        to the Great Savior
When they go to the mosque, I go with them and kneel
        before the Merciful One
When they go to some monastery, I go with them and
        reflect on Nirvana
I don't see any difference between the Gita, Bible, Koran,
        Dhammapad and scores of other Holy Scriptures
Because I find the same destination in all of them,
        regardless of disparity in avenues to reach there
I feel proud in the glorious history of all people in this
        world
I know our civilization is the sum total of all our pasts
We are the evolutionary product of all cultures and
        traditions
To me each and every part of this earth is equally holy
Each and every river is equally sacred
Each individual in himself is a pilgrimage
And the Soul residing in each of them is my God

BILLOWING BLACK CLOUDS

From the crematorium
Where the innocent in the tens of millions
Were cremated,
Only to propitiate the Spirit Evil,
Black clouds are billowing
The Evil as if metamorphosing itself
Into black clouds,
Is threatening to metastasize
Across the globe
With its insatiate urge
For devouring human soul and conscience,
It is likely to turn our beautiful world,
Resounding with free and fragrant air,
Into Hades of dehumanizing nightmares
Myopic few,
As though infatuated with its feigned cool,
Seem desperate
To live under its dark shadow,
Instead of relishing the indivisible light of sun
But to beleaguered mankind,
It is just like the invasive growth of cancer cells
An ominous presage
Of ubiquitous dust clouds,
Responsible for the onset of ice age,
Some 65 million years ago
How can humanity forget

The subsequent apocalypse,
Causing the extinction
Of precious lives
On earth?

October, 2020

LET BIRDS FLY

Let birds fly
In the open sky
Don't try to confine them

Let them dilly dally
In the vast space
Don't try to restrain them

Let them speak
To the wind
Don't try to muzzle them

BORN FREE

I was born free
I will die free
As long as
I am alive
I will breathe free

PEARLS IN OYSTER SHELLS

Once I felt like writing a poem
On my tryst with life
"Life is just like oyster shells,"
Said my Soul
So I started rummaging in them
And collected a surfeit of beautiful pearls
No matter how much I gathered
I found them outweighed by their ugly shells
Perhaps the ecstasy of life is also entrapped,
And outweighed by agony
Just like pearls in oyster shells

"THOU SHALT NOT FEAR DEATH"

One late afternoon,
Suddenly the sky roared
And a divine voice said to a man,
Standing on the shore of the ocean,
"Thou shalt not fear death
Nor shalt thou disdain life
O man,
I have made thee in my own image
And put my Soul in thee
Thy shadow will always remind thee
Of thy power that nothing can destroy
Look, along with the decline of sun
How thy shadow is stretching
It must remind thee
Of thy unceasing expansion into infinity
O man,
Thy shadow is none other than my own emissary
Who keeps reminding thee
Of my eternal presence in thy Soul"

KEEP ON PRONOUNCING

O my Soul,

Keep on pronouncing the gospels

That echo the voice of Krishna, Buddha, Jesus and
Muhammad

And many many seers, sages, prophets, and messiahs

Whose blood, vision and sacrifice

Have always nourished human civilization

O my Soul,

Keep on pronouncing the gospels

That echo the rhythm and notes of the primeval music

The Self-Existent had played while defining the
universe and our existence

TRY NOT TO FOOL YOURSELF

Dear fellow beings,
Try to invoke the power
Latent within yourself
Without which you can't see
Even if you have eyes, and
You can't hear
Even if you have ears
You need not be aligned
With any power, ideology or organization
Align yourself with your own conscience
No power on earth can hide the truth
Truth always reveals itself
Try not to fool yourself
By obscuring the sun with palms

October, 2020

NOT A WHIM

Not only life but also death
Shall always bolster my faith
We are but a superb dream
Not a whim of Reaper Grim

A journey that never ends
With hilarious twists and bends
Life, a blessing on earth indeed
Nothing its beauty can supersede

Let's enjoy it, enjoy it
To its fullest, lets' enjoy it
Let's waste not our precious time
Drink its glamor and beauty sublime

TYRANNY WILL KNEEL

Propitiate
The pen of courage
With truth and righteousness
Peace will prevail

Consecrate
The sword of boldness
With will and determination
Tyranny will kneel

JUST LEARN

"Just learn to take life
As it is," said my Soul
"Life is both
Pleasure and pain
Heat and cold
Victory and defeat
"Even death is a part of life
"Because both life and death
Are my shadows"

WHOM SHALL I ASK?

Why is our
Happiness fluid,
And misery solid?

Why is
Fullness full
And void void?

Why does
The sky cherish
Black clouds?

Why does
The thunder
Whine?

Why is
The moon
So coy?

Why does
The moon hide
Behind clouds?

Why can't
I forget my
Past?

Why is
Smile so
Pleasing?

What is
The language
Of love?

Dazzling
Multiplicity,
An illusion?

Why does
He
Create us?

What is more
Powerful, destiny
Or karma?

What is the
Relation between
Karma and fate?

How can a pendulum
Dance without the
Blessing of time?

When will
Our shadow start
Talking to us?

How deep
Is the ocean of
Human heart?

Why does our
Shadow always
Accompany us?

Shall we ever
Be the masters
Of ourselves?

Who am I
To defy the diktat
Of destiny?

The world
Of appearance,
A mirage?

O my Soul,
Why art thou
So elusive?

Do cactuses
Envy the beauty
Of rose?

Why is
Fragrance of beauty
So erotic?

JUST LIKE FOSSILS

I don't want
To evaporate like camphor
Just like fossils in rocks
I want to be inscribed
On hearts of fellow beings
For millions and millions of years
I want fellow humans
To cherish the melody
Of my gospel
In their Soul

LET ME EXPERIENCE DEMOCRACY

O America,
Let me experience Democracy,
Unalloyed, pure and pristine
I don't want its body
Encumbered by aliens' debt
Its senses salivating
For enemies' blandishments
Its mind desperate
To prostrate before foreign masters
Its intellect reeking of
Extra territorial conspiracy
And its Self operating
As evil incarnate
I want to see its character incorruptible
And its integrity intact

November, 2020

I CAN'T SEE

O my Soul,
I can't see politics
Reduced to a sordid game
Of revenge and retribution
I can't see democracy
Relegated to a plaything
At the hands of alien powers
I can't see freedom
Dismissed as a fantasy
Harbored by the disillusioned
I can't see liberty
Degraded as something
Dispensable and insignificant
I want to see their faces
Reflected in the Soul of people
Pristine, ebullient and vibrant

O PRIESTS OF DEMOCRACY AND FREEDOM!

O priests of democracy and freedom,
We know
How corrupt your priesthood is, and
How degenerate your order
How malicious your intent is, and
How depraved your ardor
Your liturgies smack of conspiracy, and
Your rituals replete with horror
You peddle nothing,
But bigotry, superstition and fanaticism
Pretending as a mediator,
In the innocent you inculcate parasitism
We know
How slavish Pharisees, Scribes and Sadducees
Keep us in the dark
Only to hide your abhorrent hideousness
We know
Who your Pontius Pilate is
And how you are going to plead before him
For the crucifixion of our cause
O clergy of democracy and freedom,
We don't need your pontification to realize our freedom
Neither do we cherish your exegesis to exercise
        democracy

The spirit of the Constitution and the Declaration of
Independence is enough to inspire us
Don't ever dare trample on it
We detest your patronage, and disdain your
condescension

November, 2020

LET'S EXPLORE THE BRIGHT NEW WORLD

Dear fellow beings,
Let's travel beyond the dark horizon of politics
And explore the bright new world
Of peace and harmony,
Fellowship and brotherhood
Let's jettison ourselves
Out of the poisonous echo chamber,
Reverberating with malice and hatred, revenge and
      retribution
Let's explore a heavenly realm
Where we can exercise our free will
Without being threatened by unscrupulous forces
Where we will not get persecuted
For having listened to the voice of our own conscience
Where we can live as human beings with full dignity
      and honor
Regardless of our creed and color, race and religion,
      ethnicity and origin, ideology and faith
Let's explore a bright new world
Where purity of Soul and the sanctity of human
      existence are most celebrated
And freedom and liberty forever upheld

November, 2020

COMPETING TO ELOPE

As if impressed
By the brimming virility
Lurking behind the impetuousness
Of swashbuckling wind,
Autumnal leaves of different hues
Seem competing
To elope with Nature's Casanova
Poor trees and plants
Divested as they are
Of their beauty and fragrance,
Following routine molestation
By ruthless time,
Plunge into lovelorn desolation

INCARCERATED
FOR CENTURIES

It is raining for several days
Temperature has sharply gone down
My surroundings are overwhelmed by snow
It is a moment of utmost despair

I am frigid, so are my emotions
I see homeless people scavenging warmth
I can feel their agony, but
I cannot share their trauma
I find myself helpless

The Almighty seems emotionless
Destiny is devoid of feelings
Fate is cruel and ruthless

Millions and millions of people are crying
They are searching for their own existence
They cannot laugh and be merry
They are deserted by their own smile

Victims to endemic darkness,
They cannot see the light
They have lost their vision
Their lives reduced to squalor

To them God is the fantasy of elites,
Religion obsolescence, and
Temples, mosques and churches
Dilapidated symbols of archaism

The ray of divinity cannot penetrate
The monolith of their solitary confinement
Incarcerated incommunicado for centuries
Neither God can listen to them
Nor can they hear His voice

March, 2006

PRAY LEAD ME

O my Soul,
Pray lead me to pure awareness
Where there is
Neither light nor dark
Neither truth nor untruth
Neither life nor death

Pray lead me to the state of unity
Where there is
Neither beginning nor end
Neither cause nor effect
Neither existence nor non-existence
Neither manifest nor unmanifest

Pray lead me to pure consciousness
Where I can
See without looking
Talk without speaking
Hear without listening, and
Walk without moving

Pray lead me to the realm supreme
Where I can
See the entire universe within me, and
Myself spread across the vast universe

O my Soul,
Pray lead me to the Absolute where
There is none, and nothing
Other than you, and
Only you

PLIGHT OF A WIDOW

The life of a widow
Is a blank paper on which
Is written the story of agony
With the ink of wind and tempest

Empty both from within and without,
She is always tormented by nothingness
That threatens to swallow her every moment

In a split second she finds herself raped
Thousands of times by marauding eyes
Who will listen to her plaintive cry
Soaked in profuse blood and tears?

Afraid of the cruelty of past, and
The ruthlessness of the present,
She can hardly face the future
With her emotions violently throttled,
She gasps for a morsel of life

March, 2004

*(An allusion to the mournful story of an illiterate, traditional village
woman whose life was devastated in the wake of her husband's
slaughter at the hands of radical Maoists in Nepal)*

MEDITATION

Isn't meditation
A full-fledged explosion
Of spiritual libido?

Om!
Om Mane Padme Hum!
Aham Brasmashmi!
Tattwamasi!
Vibrations of meditation!

How can you propitiate Shiva
Unless you meditate on phallus,
Supposedly the symbol
Of infinite cosmic power?

Donning a wreathe of human heads
Around her neck,
Four-armed, naked Kali,
Stands on the body of supine Shiva
An extremely livid Hindu goddess,
With her protruding tongue
Sipping human blood

Nudity, phallus, vagina, and
Scores of symbols,
Representing procreation
Constitute the cosmic paraphernalia
Of deities' transcendental meditation

The process of creation
Begins from the climax of bliss
Perhaps bliss and creation are one and the same
But different dimensions of meditation

March 2006

NEVER SHALL I CEASE
TO ENLIGHTEN

O my Soul,
It is solely under your command
That I have embarked on this mission

By grace of yours,
I am not afraid of any powers,
No matter how puissant
I don't submit to any authority
No matter how powerful

Every moment of my life
Is a conflagrant revolution
Each and every breath of mine
Is the revelation of absolute truth

O my Soul,
By grace of yours,
I know I am none but you,
Pure consciousness;
Luminous, eternal and immortal

Like *Uddalaka*,
Never shall I cease
To enlighten human beings
With the immortal message:
Tattwamasi, tattwamasi, tattwamasi!

ONE WITH HER

Life is not only the summit of a mountain,
But also the depth of an ocean
From where I can't fathom the universe
That always overwhelms me
With unimaginable mystique

Had it been the Elysian nectar
Sipping from love of my beloved,
I would have gulped it at a go, and
Enjoyed its intoxication

Had it been my beloved
I would have embraced her
And dissolved myself into her Being,
To instantly become one with her

SOMETIMES I DIVE DEEP ...

Sometimes I dive deep into my past,
And excavate the enthralling vestiges
Of memory, hidden somewhere
In the dark alleys of my mind

Sometimes I get inclined as a voyeur
To peep into the seductive romance,
Stemming from my liaison with
The mesmerizing phenomenal world

Sometimes I feel elated
To find myself lost
In the journey towards nothingness
That best defines
The purpose and meaning of life

JUST LIKE A BUMBLEBEE

Just like a bumblebee,
consumed with
inveterate passion,
keeps buzzing
around a flower,
we tend to revel
in the aroma and beauty
of multiplicity,
defining the attributes
of the manifest.

CENTRAL MESSAGE OF MY CHERISHED BOOK

These days
I don't want to
read any books
whether
they are
sidewalk bestsellers
or narratives
of great scholars.
I am scared,
I might be morphed
into a benighted bull
or a sensuous pig.
Equally
afraid I am
of losing my conscience
and of being
enslaved by someone's
prejudiced judgment.
These days
books seem to
have lost their
luster and fragrance
due to
insensitivity to
their own integrity
and dignity.
They seem to be
reduced to inanimate
mannequin,

devoid of mind
and conscience,
obsessed only with
cosmetic beauty
and synthetic appearance.
How can
mere collection of
words and sentences
be called a book?
In order for it
to be a book
it must be live
and vibrant,
potent enough to
rejuvenate our latent spirit,
and reinvigorate our Soul.
Truly speaking,
even my faith
in scriptures
seems dwindling.
Instead of
imparting true knowledge,
they appear
spewing platitudes
and refrains,
aimed at decimating
the core of spirituality.
Exegeses are
replete with bias
and prejudice, essentially
meant for benumbing
human spirit.
Apocryphal accounts

and concocted narratives
have obscured
the sanctity of scriptures,
thus turning them
into antiquated fossils
that
deserve only
to be placed at museums.
Scriptures and
holy books
are normally expected
to promote peace,
harmony, unity
and cooperation in
human society.
They seem to be
unleashing
chaos and confusion,
terror and bloodshed,
instead.
How long
can human society
be kept hostage
to archaic and fossilized
interpretation
of scriptures and
holy books?
Isn't it time
that our existence
got redefined
in terms of our own
genius and ingenuity,
rooted

in objective
realities of the present
and dispassionate
reminiscences of the past?
Isn't it time
that the entire process
of our thinking
got reinvented
in terms of our spontaneous
response to the
ever flowing events
and occurrences,
underlying our existence,
both physical
and spiritual?
To me
human spirit is the
best book
probably ever written
by the Being Supreme.
In it
we can read
past, present and future,
without being enslaved
by someone's
warped disposition
and convoluted veracity.
It also contains
the basic ingredients,
nourishing our existence.

O humans,
I want to see

your face in the moon,
empathetic, soothing
and radiant with
eternal hope and optimism.
I want to see
your persona
in unfathomable oceans,
calm, solemn and
all-embracing.
I also want
to see your existence
in devastative tsunamis,
ever swirling with
gigantic waves
and enormous power,
desperate to sweep
the arrogance, hubris, anomalies,
inequities and distortions,
permeating
the obdurate,
and tyrannical landscapes.
I know,
books can morph themselves
into celestial harbingers
of new realities,
depending on their
purity,
dripping from
the Soul of Time.
O fellow humans,
I want to read that book
in your Being.
I want to read that book

in the eternal reality,
underlying
your phenomenal existence.

O my Soul,
unfold thy book
in which
I can read the destiny
of my fellow beings,
fascinating, bright and ebullient.
O my Soul,
roll out thy scroll
in which
I can spy the horizon
of my fellow beings
expanding
across the last shore
of the cosmos.
Plants, shrubs, trees,
hills, mountains, plateaus,
prairies, plains,
brooks, streams, rivers and oceans,
all are colorful images
of thy book.
Human endeavor and ingenuity,
creativity and imagination,
will and determination,
renunciation and sacrifice,
are all beautiful pages
of thy book.
Human aspiration
to command the forces of Nature
by transcending

time, space and causality
is the basic character
of thy book.
Unyielding human spirit
to identify himself
with thy effervescent persona
is the central message
of thy book.
O my Soul,
I find the universe
constantly reverberating
with thy ubiquitous melody.
I see
entire lives on earth
dancing to the rhythm, and notes
of thy eternal benediction.

I am proud of humanity,
a magnificent mosaic
of variegated
color, creed, race, religion,
gender, ethnicity and origin.
Humanity
is the divine garden
where beautiful flowers
of love, compassion, empathy,
altruism, cooperation and coexistence
bloom,
with their empyrean fragrance
permeating
human relations with
entire living beings
and the planet

we live in.
How accomplished
the Sculptor Supreme is!
How consummate
the Artist Divine is!
How magnificent his creations are!
Rivers flow.
The wind blows.
Flowers bloom.
Birds sing.
Sun rises and sets.
The moon shines.
And stars twinkle.
Mountains remain steadfast,
oceans calm and serene.
Scorched deserts display
exemplary endurance.
Like children,
brooks frolic.
Celestial bodies
move and dance without
defying decorum.
Who is it
under whose command
dramatis personae
of the universe
get engaged in
their designated chores,
with utmost loyalty,
if not Him?
What a gorgeous perfection!
What an amazing completeness!
There is no emptiness

that is not full.
There is no fullness
that is not empty.
Real and unreal
enjoy playing eternal
game of hide and seek.
O my Soul,
series of mirages and illusions
strive to obscure
the true nature of reality.
They try to hoodwink
us into believing
that there is nothing
beyond the world of appearance,
and that
the search for truth
is only a wild goose chase.

O my fellow beings,
come on,
let's embark on a journey
that leads us
beyond our senses, mind and intellect.
Let's explore
the world of true knowledge
where our intuitive faculty
starts frolicking
with the realization
that we are the cosmos
unto ourselves.
Let's see the communion
between relativity and quantum
in the single unified

theory of Consciousness Supreme.
Lets' enjoy
the enigmatic dance
of entanglements
in the theater
of the Being Supreme.
Let's go surfing
on the waves,
swirling in the sea of
our transcendental existence.
Born to savor
the fruit of immortality,
we are all entitled
to pristine happiness,
ensuing from undying bond
among fellow beings.
Let's cease
to be judgmental
and start listening to
the melody of silence
within ourselves.
In that silence
we can hear
the voice of the Supreme
whose
overflowing benediction
escorts us
across the dark ocean
of separateness.
Undisturbed
by mischievous machinations
of mind and ego,
we enter

the ethereal realm
of unity
where there will be nothing,
neither we, nor the universe.
Yet there will be everything.
We not as tiny creatures,
bogged down
in the eternal cycle of
birth and death,
but as the omnipotent master
of the cosmos,
reveling in the Elysian land
of fullness and plenitude.
What an enigmatic paradox!
How grand a redemption!

If a tiny fish
in the Pacific Ocean
gets sick,
it is probable that
human civilization itself
might be jeopardized.
If a tree
in the Central Park
of New York
gets withered and wizened,
it is possible that
humanity might be
endangered.
If the glacier
in the Mount Everest area
changes its course,
incumbent administration

of the United States,
the most powerful country
on earth,
might start dwindling.
Certainly sounds absurd,
but this is the reality.
Maybe it is not possible
for us to fathom
connections,
governing the objects
and incidents in the cosmos.
How can a finite man
comprehend the
the mysteries
of cosmic infinitude?
We are too tiny
to reckon the
infinite vastness of the universe.
Isn't it amazing
that we are trying to
explore the invisible
world of sub-atomic particles
to understand
the underlying reality
of the vast and infinite cosmos?
Doesn't it mean
that there must be
some sort of inexorable
connection between the supernovas
that had exploded
billions of years ago, and
the Higgs boson?
Even a tiny ant

crisscrossing the sidewalk
of 16 Pennsylvania Avenue
can be traced to
the big bang
that occurred some
fourteen billion years ago.
Each and every thing in the cosmos,
including ourselves,
is a function of interdependence
and interconnectedness.
Nothing can be
explained in isolation.
Neither can anything
jettison itself
out of this all-encompassing
cosmic net.
Ishavasyamidam sarbam ...
When a Tibetan
commits self-immolation
in protest
seven billion people on earth
start suffering untold agony.
When a poet,
at the Chinese prison,
is subjected to
torture and death,
conscience of entire mankind
gets unprecedentedly shocked.

True,
the world is
a beautiful poetry,
with captivating rhythm,

and engrossing notes,
written on the pages of infinity
by the Being Supreme,
using the magic quill of eternity,
with consciousness as indelible ink.
Each and every word
of the poetry
represents the vibration
and vibe of its Soul.
Although part of the whole
they are the whole in themselves.

The light of moon
and the twinkling
of stars evoke
transcendental ebullience
within us.
Gentle whisper
of the wind
and rustling of leaves
throw us into
an ethereal realm.
Undulating waves,
adorning the bosoms
of oceans,
trigger within us
a different dimension
of consciousness.
Chirping of birds
and the murmur of rivers
inspire us to plunge
into the melody of
our existence.

How do these
objects of Nature,
with their characteristic
traits, make us
dive into our own Being,
and enjoy its
unparalleled exuberance?
Is it mere a coincidence,
or the paroxysmal realization
of our cosmic relations
with Nature,
and its divine mentor?

Enamored with
the hypnotic beauty
of the celestial entity,
oceans rise to embrace
moon.
Undulating waves
of the ocean,
as if pressed
by amorous passion,
enjoy playing footsie
with the shores.
Peaks of the mountain
blush at the
flirting of nascent sun.
As if infatuated
by the celestial hero's
majestic persona,
planets, too, enjoy dancing
round the sun.
Nubile vines

strive to quench
their amatory thirst
by embracing the trees,
and their branches.
Smitten with
its cosmic personality,
plants and trees,
with expectant eyes,
seem fixated
on the sky.
Once they feel spurned
by the heavenly
Casanova,
subsumed as it seems
in the romantic revelry
with celestial beauties,
they seek solace
diving into
the affectionate
embrace of mother earth.
What is this all,
if not organic thirst
instilled by Nature
in its creations?
Is it Nature's
selfish ploy to savor
vicarious pleasure,
or her
solemn intention
to promote harmony,
by creating an
unavoidable attachment
among her creations?

What is truth,
and what is untruth?
In the infinite canvas
of time and space,
there exists neither
truth nor untruth.
Just like matter
and energy are one
and the same,
so are truth and untruth.
There is no any center
on the basis of which can we measure
the radius and circumference of
truth and untruth.
The distinction
between truth and untruth
is but the projection
of circumscribed mind
of finite entities,
that we are.
Once we elevate ourselves
to a transcendental plane,
beyond the compass
of finitude,
the dividing line
between truth and untruth
simply seems blurred.
What is the difference
between Allied and Axis
Powers
in terms of commitment
to their respective

goals and objectives?

Normally, we tend to define
both truth and untruth
on the basis of how they
influence the order,
proportion and balance
of our limited existence,
defined as it is by
our finite comprehension
and myopic observation.
What is truth -
supernova
or the emergence
of scores of bright stars
subsequent to former's
explosion?
The same analogy
can be applied to the
dissolution of the cosmos
purportedly followed
by the next big bang.
Entire opposites such as -
heat and cold,
pleasure and pain,
victory and defeat -
that we experience in our life
are neither truth
nor untruth,
but transient shock waves
traveling across our psyche.
Afflictions of
human society set in

once we refuse to accept
this reality.

What is the measuring
rod to ascertain
the greatness in human
society?
Who is great -
a president or an ordinary
citizen,
or for that matter
a destitute or a billionaire?
Who is above whom?
Power, influence and money
are certainly something
that define the
mortal status of a human
being.
When it comes to the grave
what are supposed
to be the symbols of greatness
get reduced to nothing,
but soil.
What remains is
the memory related to
the deceased,
and that too disappears
one day in the darkness
of time's infinity.
Is there anything permanent
in this universe?
Is there anything constant
in this universe?

Nothing,
except for flux and impermanence.
There is none
who is great.
Neither is there anyone
who is small.
All humans are at the same level
both in terms of spirituality
and science,
which chooses to define us
as nothing,
but undulating waves
and dancing particles,
with probabilities dictating
their moves.
It also raises the question
of who should be
accountable to whom.
Accountability, too,
sometimes tends to
turn into an euphemistic
expression,
demanding submission
from the weak and meek.
In some societies,
so-called authorities are seen
to have used it as
a tool of repression.
Why should I
be accountable to
any corporeal entities
that have already forfeited
their right to govern,

on account of their failure
to recognize the ultimate truth
defining my true Being?
In such a situation,
forcing me into submission
is pure violence against
my person.
Certainly such excesses
deserve to be defied
accordingly.
What is it that defines
my true Being?
Each human is time
and space in himself.
Macrocosm and microcosm
are two ends
of his existential spectrum.
He is both tiny atom
and the vast universe.
He is the creation of
his own Self,
also defined as the Deity Supreme.
The world of appearance
owes its existence to his
dalliance
with modes of Nature.
There does not exist
any force that can circumscribe
the explosion of his initiatives,
that inevitably result in the
unending cycles of beginning and end
of the cosmos,
meticulously adorned

with impeccable order and harmony.
The entire process
around which eternally revolve
the cosmic cycles of
creation and destruction,
is the definition of his freedom.
And it is the same
freedom that defines
my true Being.
Just like the universe,
let our freedom keep
expanding
every moment, every second,
in direct proportion to
the expansion
of our consciousness.
Consciousness we are
and we are all constantly moving
towards the ultimate
destination -
being merged with
the Consciousness Supreme.
This is the central
message of my cherished book,
that my Soul itself is!

A TINY MOMENT
I WANT TO SPEND
WITH MYSELF

Liquid I'm
I'm going to freeze
In no time

I am wind
Freely I blow
One universe

I seem
Smitten with
Myself

I don't
Know who
I am

I am
Lost in my
Memory

Eyes cry
At the pain
Of heart

Love spews
The fragrance
Of Spring

Bumblebee
Hovering over
A nubile flower

Life mimics
The flow
Of a river

Just like a river
Life seeks its own
Destination

Trust in the
Eternal Being that
You are

Life exhilarates
At the tryst with
Serendipity

Life is a
Pendulum dancing to
The tune of time

Innovation is born
Out of defiance
Of conventions

Life is an
Eternal odyssey
Into mystery

Moon blushing
From behind its veil
Tumescent ocean

Dark is too
Shy and coy to
Face light

Dark
Can't stand
The flirting of light

Light seems
Desperate to see
The beauty of dark

Heart knows
The semantics
Of Soul

From Soul
Flows the stream
Of love

My shadow
Doesn't seem happy
With me

Universe in
The head of a
Tiny sparrow

Leaves in

Autumn elope
With wind

Mountain peaks
Blush at the touch
Morning sun

Clouds enjoy
Playing footsie
With wind

Dark is not
As dark as we
Think it is

Waves of ocean
Desperate to embrace
The shore

We are
The echo of our
Distant past

Nature cries
At our pain
Morning dew

Manifest
Unmanifest
Illusion

Let me
Dissolve in

My Self

A kite going
Astray in the sky
Dark horizon

Two friends
Console each other
Torrential rain

Sidewalks strewn
With autumnal foliage
Challenges galore

Matter is spirit
Spirit matter
Entanglement

Morning breeze
Stroking my inner being
Bliss ineffable

Rays of sun
Mysteries galore
Unfathomable

Autumn leaves
Fascinated with the
Impetuous wind

Cuddling clouds
Amatory passions
Staring Sphinx

Science
Smiles at our
Ingenuity

Death is the
Pinnacle of our
Cowardice

O my Soul,
Let me dissolve
In thy calm

A mind oscillating
Between hope and despair
Seasons change

Life, a tiny moment
I want to spend
With myself

THINE IS A PYRRHIC VICTORY!

O untruth,
I do congratulate thou
On thy victory
Not with warmth of heart
But with the rage of tears
Overflowing with
Anguish and indignation
At thy awful collusion
With evil
Thine is a pyrrhic victory!

Printed in the United States
By Bookmasters